ROUTLEDGE LIBRARY EDITIONS:
ARTIFICIAL INTELLIGENCE

Volume 1

THE COMPUTER SIMULATION OF BEHAVIOUR

THE COMPUTER SIMULATION OF BEHAVIOUR

MICHAEL J. APTER

Routledge
Taylor & Francis Group
LONDON AND NEW YORK

First published in 1970 by Hutchinson & Co. (Publishers) Ltd

This edition first published in 2018
by Routledge
2 Park Square, Milton Park, Abingdon, Oxon OX14 4RN

and by Routledge
711 Third Avenue, New York, NY 10017

Routledge is an imprint of the Taylor & Francis Group, an informa business

British Library Cataloguing in Publication Data
A catalogue record for this book is available from the British Library

ISBN: 978-0-8153-8566-0 (Set)
ISBN: 978-0-429-49236-5 (Set) (ebk)
ISBN: 978-1-138-49660-6 (Volume 1) (hbk)
ISBN: 978-1-351-02102-9 (Volume 1) (ebk)

Publisher's Note
The publisher has gone to great lengths to ensure the quality of this reprint but points out that some imperfections in the original copies may be apparent.

Disclaimer
The publisher has made every effort to trace copyright holders and would welcome correspondence from those they have been unable to trace.

THE COMPUTER SIMULATION OF BEHAVIOUR

Michael J. Apter
Lecturer in Psychology
University College of South Wales, Cardiff

HUTCHINSON UNIVERSITY LIBRARY
LONDON

HUTCHINSON & CO (*Publishers*) LTD
178–202 Great Portland Street, London W1

London Melbourne Sydney
Auckland Johannesburg Cape Town
and agencies throughout the world

First published 1970

This book has been set in Times type, printed in Great Britain on smooth wove paper by Anchor Press, and bound by Wm. Brendon, both of Tiptree, Essex

ISBN 0 09 102720 9 (cased)
0 09 102721 7 (paper)

TO CLAUDIE

CONTENTS

ACKNOWLEDGMENTS

I should like to thank Professor George Westby of the Department of Psychology, University College Cardiff who, in his dual roles of editor of the series and head of the department in which I work, gave me every possible help and encouragement in the writing of this book. I also wish to thank Dr John Wilson of the same department for his critical reading of the manuscript and for his valuable comments. In addition my thanks are due to Mr Alvin Lewis for his help in preparing the diagrams and to Dr A. L. Samuel of Stanford University for reading part of Chapter 4. Finally, I want to express my gratitude to all those students with whom I discussed the topic of computer simulation during the writing of this book, and whose ideas and criticisms were a continual source of stimulation.

I should like to thank: Dr R. Oldenbourg Verlag for permission to base Fig. 11 on a diagram in the paper 'GPS, A Program that Simulates Human Thought' by A. Newell and H. A. Simon, published in *Lernende Automaten*, 1961; *Scientific American* for permission to base Fig. 14 on a line drawing in the article 'Pattern Recognition by Machine' by G. Selfridge and U. Neisser, August, 1960, issue no. 203; the McGraw-Hill Book Co. for permission to base Figs. 15 and 16 on figures in *Computers and Thought* (Eds. E. A. Feigenbaum and J. Feldman), 1963; Mr A. Michael Noll for permission to reproduce his computer generated 'Composition with Lines' and Dr Margaret Masterman of the Cambridge Language Research Unit and Mr Peter Townsend of Studio International for permission to reproduce two 3-line poems which appeared in *Cybernetic Serendipity*, July 1968.

WHAT THIS BOOK IS ABOUT

It is a commonplace of popular journalism that we are entering the computer age—the age of the 'electronic brain'. So accustomed have we now become to this notion that it comes as something of a shock to realise how recent this development is and how unforeseen it generally was before it happened, especially since there is hardly any aspect of our society which will not be influenced profoundly, if it has not already been.

This book is about the use of computers in just one area—psychology. Furthermore, it is about only one use of computers within psychology. It is neither about computer data processing, nor the computer control of experiments, although both these techniques are interesting and valuable in their own right. What this book *is* about is a technique which takes fairly seriously the 'electronic brain' epithet, and which may in the long term prove even more important to psychology and through psychology to society as a whole: the computer modelling of psychological processes.

This text is intended as a non-technical introduction to a rapidly developing, and in some respects highly technical, subject and to the problems which it encompasses. Within this overall objective a number of aims will be pursued concurrently.

The first aim is to examine how far one can accept the 'mechanist' hypothesis in psychology—the hypothesis that man is a machine and that his behaviour should therefore be studied accordingly. One way of doing this, the way adopted in this book, is to try to see if there is any kind of human behaviour which could not be accomplished by a machine like a digital computer. If there is not, then one could argue that unless further evidence is forthcoming it would indeed be most economical theoretically to regard man as a machine.

The second aim of the book is to evaluate the usefulness of computer simulation as a technique to be used by psychologists in their attempt to increase their understanding of behaviour. To this end some particular representative computer models of particular aspects of behaviour, or processes underlying behaviour, are studied in sufficient detail to allow of critical discussion. The models described were chosen either because they were deemed to be classics or because they were judged to be fairly typical contributions in their respective fields. The preponderance of American work among that described may be regarded as unpatriotic, but it can hardly be denied that the Americans have dominated this aspect of computer technology almost as much as they have dominated computer technology in general.

The third aim is to indicate briefly, without attempting an exhaustive review—which is in any case not possible within the confines of a book of this length—the range of computer models of behaviour which have been constructed to date. In this respect, it is also intended to show how the field of computer simulation relates to other fields of study.

Should the reader wish to enquire further about computer simulation models or, as they are sometimes called, '*information processing models*', he is referred first to the references which are given as footnotes within each chapter. These references are, in the main, to papers, and wherever a paper has been published in more than one place an attempt has been made to give the most generally accessible reference. Secondly, at the end of each chapter a list is given of books which are related to the subject-matter of the chapter (although many of them deal with a wider area than the chapter itself does). These selected references are recommended for further reading. A comparatively small number of books deal with more or less the whole area covered in this book. Although most of these are individually recommended at the end of chapters to which they are particularly relevant, they are also listed in a special reference section at the end of the book (together with a paper which surveys the field).

It is hoped that this book about computers will be of interest to students of psychology and philosophy, the general reader and, who knows, perhaps also one day to computers.

I

BRAINS, COMPUTERS AND MODELS

THE MAN-MACHINE ANALOGY

There are two related ideas concerning men and machines. The first is that machines can be built with the same functional capacities as men; the second is that men are not only like, but really are, complex machines. Neither of these ideas are entirely new and they date from long before the advent of the computer.

The possibility of an artificial man has obsessed men through the ages, from the obscure medieval idea of a golem—a wooden image given life by the saints—to the horror-laden fantasy of a Frankenstein's monster, the functional twentieth-century robot and the futuristic android (which, as readers of science fiction know, is a robot which is indistinguishable from a human being).

The idea that in any case man, in common with all organisms, *is* a machine—the mechanist or anti-vitalist hypothesis—is more difficult to trace being caught up as it has been with undercurrents of thought and feeling over the centuries in science, philosophy and religion. The idea that man is a machine implies that man is *no more than* a machine and that concepts like soul, will, sin and so on are at best irrelevant and at worst totally misleading. Naturally, scientists acting as scientists have methodically disregarded concepts of this kind which do not lead to objective measurement and which are non-parsimonious in explanation. Thus they have inevitably treated man as if he were a machine. In this light the computer simulation of behaviour lies in the main stream of scientific thought, although it perhaps implies a more blatantly mechanistic attitude to the human brain and human behaviour than is usually found in the biological sciences.

Oddly enough, the attitude of the modern scientist is in one respect similar to that of primitive man: men and machines are seen as essentially alike. Primitive man being animistic like a child elevates objects to the level of men by ascribing souls to them: stones feel pain if you kick them, clouds enjoy floating in the air, boats want to move through the water. But to the scientist they are the same not because both kinds of entity have souls but because the idea of a soul serves no purpose in the study of either. Between primitive man and the scientist lies a third view which is probably still that of the symbolic 'common man' and which has been associated in western civilisation especially with Christianity. This is the view that man has a soul while objects and machines do not.

If one studies the development of the biological and psychological sciences in modern times one finds a progression from this Christian view to the view that, whether or not man does possess a soul, he can be successfully studied as if he did not. This progression has been associated with various views about what kind of machine man can most appropriately be regarded as.

In the seventeenth century Descartes, hovering uneasily between strong commitment to both Christianity and the rapidly developing science of his time, argued that animals were wholly machines and had no soul while humans were partly machine and possessed a soul.

On the basis of observations carried out during dissections and even vivisections of animals, Descartes (in his tract *De Homine*) claimed that 'vital functions' of the animal body were the result of heat and motion of liquids within the body, especially within blood vessels and nerves. In particular, he saw the nerves as hollow tubes between brain and muscles in which flowed a substance: the movement of this substance in the nerves caused the movements of the muscles and hence brought about behaviour in much the same way as the performance of various moving toys of the period was based on the use of hydraulic tubes. Animals were said to be devoid of consciousness and even thought, and to Descartes the cries of a cat being vivisected represented no more than the noise of breaking machinery.

Man, however, was believed by Descartes to be different: although in many of his functions he was like an animal and therefore mechanical, he differed in that he possessed and was governed by a soul. On this view man was able to think, control his activities and possess consciousness. Descartes even went so far as to point to an anatomic seat for the soul: the pineal gland, which is situated centrally in the brain. He had a number of reasons for choosing this location, including the apparent absence of the pineal gland in animals: its centrality, the fact that it is not doubled (like the cortex, cerebellum, etc.), and his belief based on observation that it is the centre of a network of nerve endings which act upon it and which it in turn acts upon: '. . . the machine of the body is so formed that from the simple fact that this gland is diversely moved by the soul, or by such other cause, whatever it is, it thrusts the spirits which surround it towards the pores of the brain, which conduct them by the nerves into the muscles, by which means it causes them to move the limbs.'[1] Descartes also argued that the pineal gland exerted its influence not by altering the *amount* of motion of the 'spirits' in the nerves but by altering their *direction.*

The argument was spoiled not long after by the discovery by the Danish scientist Niel Stenson of the pineal gland in animals.[2] More significantly it appeared that Descartes' notion of the activity of the soul contradicted Newton's Third Law of Motion and the related Law of Conservation of Momentum. The effect of these laws is that the total quantity of motion in the universe in any given direction is constant, as well as its total amount being constant.

In the next century La Mettrie, the French philosopher, took Descartes' argument to its logical conclusion: if animals are machines then men are machines too. In his book *L'Homme Machine* (1748) he argued that '. . . man is but an animal, or a collection of springs which wind each other up. . . . If these springs differ among themselves, these differences consist only in their position and in their degrees of strength, and never in their nature; wherefore the soul is but a principle of motion or a material and sensible part of the brain, which can be regarded, without fear of error, as the mainspring of the whole machine, having a visible influence on all the parts.'[3] This materialist view is perhaps a direct antecedent of modern 'behaviourism' with its emphasis on what the organism *does* and its (at least methodological) disregard for consciousness. La Mettrie

[1] Article XXXIV of the First Part of 'The Passions of the Soul', trans. Haldane, Elizabeth S., and Ross, G. R. T., in *The Philosophical Works of Descartes* (Cambridge University Press, 1911).

[2] Butterfield, Herbert, *The Origins of Modern Science* (London, Bell, 1951), p. 111.

[3] La Mettrie, Julien Offray de, *Man a Machine*, English trans., annotated by Bussey, G. C. (La Salle, Illinois, Open Court Publishing Company, 1953), p. 135.

used the term 'machine' quite broadly and gave consideration to chemical as well as purely mechanical processes in the body.

Not long afterwards another French philosopher, Abbé de Condillac,[1] took up the man-machine idea by considering a statue which is, in fantasy, given one after another all the senses that man possesses. Condillac used this fiction, which would probably have been inconceivable at an earlier date, to consider the way in which an entity can come to have knowledge of its own body and of objects outside its body, and what the limitations of knowledge are. In a sense he is a forerunner of cybernetics (see Chapter 2) since he examines the logical properties of 'systems' without regard to whether they are 'living' or not.

Although the machine model of man is not paraded so obviously in the nineteenth century[2] the human organism, including the brain, is already being treated scientifically by physiologists as a machine. It has been pointed out[3] that the major emphasis of this physiological study during the nineteenth and well into the twentieth century is on questions of energy utilisation, the organism being regarded as an engine for converting food into more living matter or into activity. The activity of the nervous system is also seen mainly in this context; that is, the body is studied in terms of physics and chemistry, but not in terms of its logical organisation or its information utilisation.

Early in the present century another way of looking at the brain became popular in the newly emerging discipline of scientific psychology: this was the idea that it acts rather like a self-operating telephone switchboard connecting up sensory inputs with motor outputs in different patterns. In this view, learning involves connecting inputs and outputs in new combinations (or in some sense strengthening connections already in existence) and forgetting involves disconnecting inputs and outputs that have previously been connected (or in some sense weakening the connection). This analogy between the brain and a telephone switchboard was stated explicitly by writers such as Pearson[4] and was at least implicit in the ideas of major figures such as Sherrington in England,

[1] Condillac, Étienne Bonnot, Abbé de, *Traité des Sensations* (1754), English trans. *Treatise on Sensations* by Carr, Geraldine (London, Favil Press, 1930).

[2] A 'steam man' was, however, built towards the end of the century. See Asimov, Isaac, 'The perfect machine', in *Science Journal*, special issue on *Machines like Men*, **4**, 10 (October 1968), pp. 115–18.

[3] Wiener, Norbert, *Cybernetics* (New York, Wiley, 1948), ch. 1.

[4] Pearson, K., *The Grammar of Science* (London, Black, 2nd ed., 1900, reprinted in Everyman's Library, London, Dent, 1937).

Thorndike in America and Pavlov in Russia. This theory had its roots in the associationist philosophy so beloved by generations of British philosophers and is still a force in modern psychology.

Finally, in the progress of the man-machine analogy to date, the development of the modern computer has led to the conception of the nervous system as a type of general-purpose computer.

It could be said, cynically, that our attempt to understand the brain is based at any time on the characteristics of the most advanced machines in use at that time. Descartes, La Mettrie and other thinkers of the seventeenth and eighteenth centuries conceptualised the nervous system in terms of clocks, music boxes, water toys, and automata of the period like dancing ballerinas. Scientists of the nineteenth century thought in terms of steam engines, and early in the twentieth century in terms of the telephone networks then coming into existence. It could be argued that it is only to be expected that the current excitement about computers should lead to a fashion for comparing the brain to a computer, the implication being that it will be overtaken in due course by another more 'modern' and up-to-date analogy. The reader will be in a better position to judge for himself whether or not this analogy is something more fundamental than a temporary fashion after reading the next section.

THE COMPUTER-BRAIN ANALOGY

Let us, then, look more closely at the analogy which is now so often drawn between the brain and a general-purpose digital computer.[1] The two kinds of system may be said to resemble each other in the following ways:

(1) Both are *general-purpose* devices. That is to say, they are both capable of dealing with a wide variety of problems whose *exact* nature cannot be anticipated, but they can temporarily assume special-purpose forms when they are dealing with particular prob-

[1] This discussion will become clearer when the chapter on digital computing has been read. A slightly more detailed introductory discussion of the computer-brain analogy which can be recommended is Sutherland, N. S., 'Machines like men' in *Science Journal*, special issue on *Machines like Men*, *4*, 10 (October 1968). Considerably more detail is to be found in a number of the books referred to at the end of this chapter.

lems. Unlike the brains of most other animals which are specialised to carry out certain particular functions, the human brain is highly flexible, especially through its ability to abstract and use language. One might say that the brain and the general-purpose computer are the two most general-purpose devices known to man. Of these two, the human brain is at present effectively more general-purpose than the computer. This book is concerned to a large extent with the question: 'How do we release the full general-purpose potential of the computer?'

(2) Both are *information processing* devices. That is, at the most general level they may both be described as receiving environmental information through input devices, manipulating this information in accordance with information already in the system (in computer terms the sequence of instructions comprising the program together with other information held in store) and returning information to the environment through output devices. For this reason computer models of particular brain processes are often called 'information processing models'. Interestingly enough, the information processed in both cases appears to be coded in binary form. In one case it is represented in terms of two-state electronic components and in the other in terms of neurons (the cells of the nervous system) which either fire (relay a pulse) or do not fire at a given moment (although recent neurophysiological research has shown that the situation may after all be more complex than this).

(3) Both may incorporate *models* within themselves. As Kenneth Craik,[1] who anticipated many of the ideas of cybernetics, pointed out, one of the fundamental functions of the brain may be to build up and use models of its environment. Among contemporary scientists, J. Z. Young[2] in particular has made much use of the idea in his work on the octopus brain. The interesting situation arises that not only can the computer model the brain, the brain can also model the computer.

(4) Both achieve their intellectual excellence by carrying out *large numbers* of *primitive operations*. As Wooldridge has said: '. . . what is really fundamental about the general types of machines that have been too narrowly described as "electronic digital computers" is that they get their amazing results by the performance of a very large number of very simple processing steps. This would

[1] Craik, Kenneth, *The Nature of Explanation* (Cambridge University Press, 1943, reprinted 1967).

[2] Young, J. Z., *A Model of the Brain* (Oxford, Clarendon Press, 1964).

also appear to be a valid description of the essence of brain function.'[1] In both cases, too, the primitive operations are carried out at high speed.

At the same time, there are a number of obvious differences between the brain and the present generation of digital computers. Despite recent advances, the size of components in the computer is still much greater than in the brain, and there are fewer of them, but the speed with which they function is far greater. Also, the brain is, unlike the digital computer, not entirely digital in its operation; thus even if the neurons are digital (discrete), the synapses, or junctions between them, are analogue (continuous) in operation. Nevertheless, differences of this kind are trivial from the point of view of the analogy which is between the organisation and logic of the two systems and not between the components they happen to utilise.

Many other differences between digital computers, at least in the way in which they are conventionally used at present, and brains, can in principle be overcome by suitable programming and the adoption of convenient conventions.

For example, computers are normally entirely sequential (serial) in their operation, although computers that carry out simultaneous operations do exist. In contrast, the brain is highly parallel in its functioning, carrying out large numbers of operations simultaneously. However, a conventional serial computer can be programmed to simulate parallel operations. Suppose a simple parallel system performs a sequence of actions $a_1, a_2 \ldots a_n$ at the same time as another sequence $b_1, b_2 \ldots b_n$, where a_1 and b_1 occur at the same time, as do a_2 and b_2 etc. A sequential system can achieve the same effect by performing a_1 followed by b_1, then a_2 followed by b_2 etc., making sure that if *a* events can effect *b* events or *vice versa*, then the result of a_1 does not effect b_1 but b_2, and so on. A sequential computer therefore can also simulate parallel systems. (Where the term 'parallel' is used in later chapters to refer to computer models, this simulation is really what is meant.) Alternatively, a number of computers could in principle be connected up to each other to operate in parallel; this is not entirely fanciful since computer networks are already coming into existence for various purposes.

Another difference between the two systems is that the computer automatically takes whatever information is fed into it, while the

[1] Wooldridge, Dean E., *The Machinery of the Brain* (New York, McGraw-Hill, 1963), p. 236.

brain to some extent selects what information it will receive by deciding what part of its environment it will come in contact with, by asking questions, and so on. The brain also filters the information which it does happen to receive at a given time, so that only a small part of the incoming information is in fact attended to. Now there is no reason why a computer too should not request certain kinds of information, as it already does in certain situations (for example, when it is being used as a teaching machine). There is also no reason why it should not be programmed to select, according to certain criteria, a subset of information to be stored from the totality of its input information, as again it already does in certain situations.

Does this mean that there are *no* fundamental differences between brains and computers? It is probably too early to answer this question with confidence until more is known about the way in which the brain operates. But there are certainly some differences which look as if they might be more radical than those mentioned so far. Thus, the fact that the brain exhibits equipotentiality in many of its areas, which the computer does not, appears to constitute a basic difference. If certain parts of the living brain are removed, the remaining parts automatically take over the functions of the parts removed. Also, learned habits appear not to be stored in particular localised neurons but to be spread in some way throughout larger areas so that extirpation of limited parts of the brain does not necessarily mean the loss of habits. By contrast, if part of the computer is damaged in any way, the result is at least the loss of the information in those parts (program or other data) and may even be the total breakdown of the whole system. It is clear that the computer contains nothing like as much redundancy (see Chapter 2) as the human brain, and therefore does not have the reserves of information to overcome the information loss and maintain reliability. But how the brain is organised to accomplish this amazing feat of equipotentiality is not at all well understood. Information in memory for example must be spread around the system in a way quite unlike the way it is stored in the computer, and methods of retrieving this information when required must also be rather different. (The fact that the brain has two cortical hemispheres which are in some respects equivalent adds a further element of mystery to the situation.)

It would clearly be advantageous if computers also were equipotential, and it is possible that one day the principles of holography will be harnessed to this end. Indeed, the brain itself may work in accordance with the same principles. (Holography is a recently developed technique for reproducing visual images in three dimensions, usually using lasers. If part of the image is destroyed, enough information is contained in the rest of the image for the whole image to be recreated, although less perfectly.) Another possibility is that organic components will be used increasingly in the fabrication of computers so that computers will have, for example, tissue-culture memory cells. One can envisage that a cheap way of building at least parts of computers would be to try to grow them, using self-reproducing cells as the basic components. It need hardly be added that this is highly speculative at the present stage. But if it could be accomplished then the difference between computers and brains would naturally be greatly reduced.

The brain appears to be reliable in another way: it functions in terms of patterns, and if some of the elements of the pattern are missing the brain in effect reconstructs them. This can be demonstrated especially in terms of perceptual patterns, a fact which the Gestalt psychologists made much of. But it also seems to be true of memory and of the sorts of thought processes which projective tests are based on, i.e. it successfully builds on reduced information. It must be more than coincidence that a system which can overcome the loss of parts which contain information can also overcome the loss of information in other ways. But the relation between physiological equipotentiality and cognitive organisation remains obscure. The computer is typically as lacking in its ability to deal with patterns as it is in its lack of ability to overcome damage and if, for example, a small piece of input information is missing or incorrect, this can make nonsense of the whole program. However, as we shall see in Chapter 6, progress *is* being made on this front and more sophisticated programming methods may allow a program to recognise and use patterns of information.

If computers are less reliable than brains, they are also more precise. Thus their capacity for precise arithmetic calculation is considerably greater than that of humans. This has led von Neumann to suggest this fundamental difference between the two kinds of system: '. . . the nervous system appears to be using a radically different system of notation from the ones we are familiar with in ordinary arithmetics and mathematics: instead of the precise systems of markers where the position—and presence or absence—of every marker counts decisively in determining the meaning of the message, we have here a system of notations in which the meaning is conveyed by the *statistical* properties of the message.' He concludes that '. . . a deterioration in arithmetics has been traded for an improvement in logics'.[1] In other words, the language used by the brain may not be the language of mathematics. But if this is true, the nature of this brain language is completely unknown to us. As Singh has said: 'In this respect we may well be as ignorant as the Greeks, who located the mind in the midriff.'[2] The discovery of the way in which this language functioned would constitute a momentous breakthrough not only from the point of view of understanding the brain, but also from the point of view of the construction of intelligent computer systems.

Although therefore there do appear to be some fundamental differences between the brain and the computer—or at least the present-day computer—several points must be made clear. The first is that this does not mean that the brain is *not* a machine; it means that it is in some respects a different kind of machine from a computer. The second is that this does not mean that the computer is no good for simulating behaviour. The computer is an excellent general purpose simulating device and can be used to simulate a wide variety of systems, e.g. business organisations, military conflict situations, etc. It may have *advantage* in simulating behaviour and the processes which underlie behaviour over all other systems it simulates in that it *does* resemble the brain in the fundamental ways outlined earlier. The question of whether the brain at the physiological level is analogous to the computer at the hardware level is interesting but not of crucial importance in this book. We are mainly concerned with the resemblance between programs, which happen to be represented for various reasons on computers but could in principle be realised in other ways, and processes, which can best be described at the psychological rather than the physiological level.

THE USE OF COMPUTER MODELS

There has been much discussion by philosophers of science about what the status of models is in science. The view adopted in this book[3] is that they are at one and the same time simplified forms of the systems which they are modelling and more concrete forms of abstract ideas. For example, a computer model of pattern-

[1] von Neumann, John, *The Computer and the Brain* (New Haven, Yale University Press, 1958), pp. 79–80.
[2] Singh, Jagjit, *Great Ideas in Information Theory, Language and Cybernetics* (New York, Dover Publications, 1966), p. 139.
[3] An attempted justification of it is given in ch. 1 of the author's *Cybernetics and Development* (Oxford, Pergamon, 1966).

recognition might be much simpler than the human pattern-recognition system which involves large numbers of interacting retinal and neuronal cells; and yet it may also function according to the same abstract principles (e.g. of classification) and the model constitutes a more concrete version of these principles. In other words, models mediate between general theories and particular systems which the theories intend to explain. Sometimes the model is derived from the theory and compared to the system being investigated, so that evaluation of the theory takes place through the model: in this case, a hypothetico-deductive system is being used in which the hypotheses deduced interact with each other in the form of a dynamic functioning model. Conversely, sometimes a model is constructed by direct analogy with the system being studied and abstract ideas are then induced. We shall return to this conception of the function of models in the next chapter in the context of cybernetics.

Of course if the term 'theory' is used in a general way to refer to any explanatory device, then one can count a model *as* a theory. Thus Simon and Newell,[1] whose work on computer simulation will be examined in Chapter 5, argue that all theories are analogies of different kinds which may be verbal or mathematical or more obviously analogical. Computer analogies in this respect are no different from those theories which may be analogies using the symbols of natural language. Nevertheless, it is still necessary to make the distinction drawn in the last paragraph between highly abstract theories, and more concrete models, using the terms 'theory' and 'model' in their most widely used senses.

It has sometimes been argued in psychology, and Skinner has been a particularly notable exponent of this point of view,[2] that theories, and by extension models, are not needed. The implication of Skinner's work is that if you can control a system (like a rat in a Skinner box) you can understand it and no further theoretical superstructure is required. However, this is patently absurd. A man might be able to ride a horse, a woman drive a car, or a child operate a television set, without any understanding in each case of how the system controlled works. The converse is also true: one might be able to understand a system without being able to

[1] Simon, Herbert A., and Newell, Allen, 'Models: their uses and limitations', in *The State of the Social Sciences,* Ed. White, Leonard D. (Chicago University Press, 1956).

[2] Skinner, B. F., 'Are theories of learning necessary?', in *Psychol. Rev.* **57**, (1950), 193–216.

control it. Thus, an astronomer might be able to understand why the planets follow the orbits they do without being able to control them. Unfortunately, then, control and understanding are not necessarily related.

When it comes to trying to understand the behaviour of a system like a human being one is faced with particularly severe difficulties. The human organism is a complex whole which processes information in terms of perceptual organisation, linguistic and other symbolic organisation, and evaluative organisation (attitude and value systems), all of these schemata interacting with each other. The organism can be regarded as a kind of dynamic Gestalt in which a change in any part may involve changes throughout the whole system. Certainly one can isolate functional relationships, as Skinner does, and use these in some measure to control the organism. But to understand behaviour fully, synthesis is needed as well as experimental analysis of the behaviourist variety. How can one synthesise to any extent even in terms of restricted psychological processes except by means of models? How, for example, can one understand how a person recognises a pattern or constructs a sentence without in some way constructing a model of this process?

Hilgard and Bower[1] point out that 'The argument has been that more complex behaviours—thinking and problem-solving—could be more easily understood once simple behaviours under especially simplified conditions were better understood. . . . After some 30 to 40 years without striking advances in our understanding of the capabilities of the human mind, this argument has begun to have a hollow ring. . . . But the computer simulation technology has given us a tool for dealing with complexity in our theories. . . .'

Theorisation must of course always be based on empirical observation in science, and this means that in psychology the evidence for theorisation must all come from the observation of overt behaviour. But this does not mean that the explanation has to be as peripheral as the observation. As Chomsky has said,[2] '. . . the term "behavioral science" suggests a not-so-subtle shift of emphasis towards the evidence itself and away from the deeper underlying principles and abstract mental structures that might be illuminated by the evidence of behavior'.

[1] Hilgard, Ernest R., and Bower, Gordon H., *Theories of Learning* (New York, Appleton-Century-Crofts, 1966), p. 424.

[2] Chomsky, Noam, *Language and Mind* (New York, Harcourt, Brace and World, 1968), p. 58.

Chomsky, in fact, has drawn a distinction in his examination of language between observed linguistic behaviour and linguistic competence which underlies this behaviour but is not realised in any direct or simple way in it. We shall look at this argument in more detail in the chapter on language. The point to be made here is that a similar argument can be applied to behaviour in general and not just linguistic behaviour. A computer program may then be a model of behavioural competence and give rise to outputs analogous to observed behaviour in the system being modelled.

If models are essentially explanatory in function, as it is argued here they are, then the criteria used to judge them must be those used to judge theories in general. One will never be able to prove that a model is 'true', just as one can never finally prove that a theory is true.[1] The most that one can say of both a theory and a model is that it is consistent with the known facts, not that it is true. However, other explanations of the same facts are always possible. Thus the same behaviour might be exhibited by models using different means. So how does one choose between computer models of the same process? Again, the answer must be: in the same way as one chooses between theories. That is to say, the preferred explanation is the one which is most parsimonious in its assumptions and economic in its expression, which encompasses more of the known facts, and which appears to be most fruitful for future research i.e. gives rise to the largest number of interesting and testable deductions. If one of the explanations is not in principle refutable, then it should be rejected as an unscientific dogma: this situation is unlikely to arise in choosing between models, since functioning models have to be precise and effective (although problems may arise about how to interpret the model, i.e. what in the model represents what in the system it is simulating).

There are many different types of models which it is possible to construct. One might, for example, construct a model in hardware form—like a molecular model in chemistry or a model aeroplane in a wind tunnel in aerodynamics. Why, in psychology, should one think in terms of models in the form of computer programs? The answer is that there are a number of advantages which computer models may have over other types of model or method of theorising in psychology. These advantages may be listed as follows:

(1) As we saw in the last section of this chapter, there is an *a*

[1] For the argument behind this statement, see Popper, Karl R., *The Logic of Scientific Discovery* (London, Hutchinson, 1959).

priori resemblance between the general purpose computer and the human brain which controls human behaviour.

(2) One is forced to consider the process one is modelling *holistically*. The importance of this will be realised if the discussion above is borne in mind.

(3) In order to write a program which works one is forced to put one's ideas in *precise* form. Much theorising in psychology, for example in the psychoanalytic tradition, is vague and ambiguous, and to this extent such theories are untestable. With computer programs one is, on the contrary, forced to state exactly what it is one is claiming about the system or process under consideration. Furthermore if one knows enough to be able to specify such a process in the step-by-step detail required for a computer program one can claim that one already knows a certain amount about it.

(4) Computer models must be *effective*: they must actually work. That is to say, the program must be both complete and also contain no hidden inconsistencies. It is probably true to say that many theories in psychology, even those which are precise, might prove not to be completely effective if put in the form of a computer program. For example, it would be interesting to know if Hull's theory was really effective. It is a necessary condition of any theory that it be effective in this sense, and embodying the theory in a computer model provides an appropriate test.

It is also of course necessary to show that the theory does work in the way expected: that is, that predictions that are made from the theory are correct deductions. With a complex theory this may not always be obvious. So a computer model based on the theory, even if effective, may not work in the way expected—if it does not, the theory requires modification just as it would if empirical facts predicted by it did not occur.[1]

(5) A computer model brings one's ideas to life and *demonstrates* them in a striking and exciting manner. Thus it is for most people more stimulating to see a computer learn to play draughts than to read a mathematical model of the same process. The end-product may well be more reinforcing for the model builder too: simulating may be stimulating. (And, let's admit it, model building of all

[1] An excellent example of this is a program by Rochester *et al.* based on Hebb's theory which showed that it did not work in the way Hebb expected: Rochester, N., Holland, J., Haibt, L., and Duda, W., 'Test on a cell assembly theory of the action of the brain, using a large digital computer', *IRE Trans. Inform. Theory* (1956), IT–2, 80–93.

kinds gives a scientist some of the pleasure of being a creative artist.)

There are also a number of disadvantages inherent in the use of computer models:

(1) The modeller is likely to become so distracted by *computer program problems per se*—like how to overcome storage limitations, or whether the program itself is sufficiently elegant—that he may lose sight of the goal of understanding the system being modelled.

One of the main causes of distraction is likely to consist of errors in the program; and unfortunately one error may be enough to vitiate the whole program. This is an advantage from the point of view of ensuring precision, but the situation can be highly frustrating and time wasting where the error is a small programming mistake which has nothing to do with the viability of the ideas being expressed: one might for example have typed one wrong number onto the program tape. Anyone who has ever tried to use a computer will know of the technical tribulations which are likely to assail one from the moment one sits in front of the tape punch machine. If at some stage in the future the computer could be programmed with a basic pattern-recognition program for receiving and interpreting other information programmed into it, then the small mistake might lose its tyrannical power. (The development of pattern-recognition programs is examined in Chapter 6.) Meanwhile the programmer must do what he can to ensure total accuracy of input information.

(2) A certain *minimum complexity* of interrelated ideas is probably necessary to make a theoretical schema worth putting in the form of a computer program. If a theoretical idea is so simple that its implications in the form of a model are obvious and entirely predictable, and the question of effectiveness does not arise, then bearing in mind the problems just described it is probably not advantageous to program it. One must in some sense try to get more out of the computer than one puts into it. This is, strictly, a limitation on the use of computers rather than a disadvantage as such.

(3) Although it may be possible to demonstrate vividly that a set of ideas work through a functioning computer program, it may be *difficult to describe* the detailed program which exemplifies these ideas. If anything like a complete description is to be given—and this is usually not possible within the space of a research paper—the reader easily becomes lost in a wealth of detail. Probably the best solution to this problem is to describe the program by means of

flow diagrams (see Chapter 3) which give an idea of the logical structure of the program, and to take special pains to make clear what the theoretical ideas underlying the program consist of.

A certain amount of expertise in computer programming may also be required by the reader, and this is perhaps the main reason why computer simulation as a technique has had less impact so far on experimental psychology than it might have done. In the long run this may not prove so much of a disadvantage, since an increasing number of researchers are in any case becoming familiar with computer programming for data processing purposes.

(4) Probably the major problem is that of how to judge how well the complex dynamic whole of the program *matches* the complex dynamic whole of the system it is modelling. This is a problem to which we shall return many times explicitly or implicitly in subsequent chapters.

The disadvantages of using computer programs, then, are substantial. Any other method of model building, however, would appear to have even greater disadvantages: natural language models cannot guarantee precision or effectiveness, hardware models are even more time-consuming to construct than computer programs, and so on. It is therefore difficult to conceive of any really satisfactory alternative to computer programming for many purposes.

This section has been about computer *simulation*. There is however a related form of computer programming which should also be mentioned: computer *synthesis*, as it is generally called. The aim of a synthesis program is to achieve a particular piece of behaviour (e.g. to solve a certain kind of problem) using any means that are suitable and convenient. This constrasts with simulation which requires not only that a certain kind of behaviour be produced but also that it be produced in the same way, as far as one can tell, as in the system being modelled. In other words, with simulation one is concerned with both means and ends, with synthesis one is concerned only with ends. In principle, if simulation is used by the pure scientist in order to try to understand a system he is studying, synthesis is used by the applied scientist in order to achieve certain practical ends, for example in industry. In practice, the situation is far less clear-cut. For example, even if the program is used primarily for the purpose of synthesis, the fact that it achieves certain ends which may also be achieved (although perhaps less well) by humans, means that the program may be a contender to be treated as a model—unless it is disqualified by using some means which is clearly quite different from those used by humans.

SELECTED REFERENCES

Braithwaite, R. B., *Scientific Explanation* (Cambridge University Press, 1964).
Cohen, John, *Human Robots in Myth and Science* (London, Allen and Unwin, 1966).
Evans, G. W., Wallace, G. F., and Sutherland, G. L., *Simulation Using Digital Computers* (New Jersey, Prentice-Hall, 1967).
George, F. H., *The Brain as a Computer* (Oxford, Pergamon, 1961).
von Neumann, John, *The Computer and the Brain* (New Haven, Yale University Press, 1958).
Wooldridge, Dean E., *The Machinery of the Brain* (New York, McGraw-Hill, 1963).
Young, J. Z., *A Model of the Brain* (Oxford University Press, 1964).

2

CYBERNETICS

INTRODUCTION

The computer simulation of behaviour has to a large extent emerged as part of a new and exciting discipline—Cybernetics. To understand the full implications and possibilities of computer simulation in psychology it is necessary to know something of this broader context, and the aim of this chapter is therefore to provide a general introduction to the subject. Fortunately, although cybernetics is a technical subject, its overall aims and many of its basic ideas are not in themselves difficult to understand.

If the idea of computers and 'electronic brains' has caused some public excitement during the last decade, the idea of 'cybernetics' is also beginning to catch the popular imagination. In fact, the word is already taking its place alongside such other fashionable avant-garde words as 'subliminal' and 'psychedelic', and no self-respecting science fiction writer will fail to use it (or its modifications, e.g. 'cybermen', 'cybermats' and 'cyborgs') wherever possible. It is still, however, something of a 'one-up' word since very few people know what it means. This is a pity because the use of the word thus becomes even more confused than it otherwise would have been —and even where it is used by the cognoscenti there are differences of emphasis which make for some ambiguity.

The word 'cybernetics' comes from the Greek 'Kybernetike' meaning, roughly, 'steersmanship'. Plato used this word to refer to the science of piloting or steering in *The Republic*. Ampère, the French physicist, re-coined the word to refer to the political art of government—in fact the word 'government' is itself derived from the Latin 'gubernator' which is in turn a corruption of the Greek word.

Finally, in 1948, Norbert Wiener, a distinguished professor of mathematics at the Massachusetts Institute of Technology, published a book entitled *Cybernetics*[1] in which he introduced the word to refer to a new inter-disciplinary subject that he felt was emerging and which took as its subject-matter control and communication systems of all kinds, i.e. self-governing or self-steering systems. Not only did Wiener do much to crystallise the formation of this new subject through the writing of this book but he was also one of its major practitioners.

Wiener's definition of cybernetics, given in the sub-title of his book, was that it was the study of 'control and communication in the animal and the machine'. Although this definition is one with which most people working in the field would still agree, the field it refers to is in principle so wide—at its widest it relates to parts of engineering, mathematics, logic, linguistics, biology, physiology, medicine, anthropology, psychology, sociology and economics among other subjects—that it is not surprising that there have been differences of emphasis. (At the same time it is this very diversity which lends to cybernetics much of its special excitement.) It is also not in itself a particularly helpful definition for someone reading about cybernetics for the first time, and to impart a feeling for the subject it is essential to give some examples of cybernetic ideas and research.

There have been many different interpretations of cybernetics and the interpretation given here is necessarily personal. It is an interpretation which, however, is wide enough to encompass all the different strands which have at some stage or another, and with varying degrees of emphasis, been regarded as belonging to cybernetics. In this broadest sense the field is perhaps the same as that to which the term 'systems research' is beginning to be applied.[2,3] If the latter term becomes more widespread and is used fairly consistently, then it will perhaps be preferable to cybernetics.

[1] Wiener, N., *Cybernetics* (New York, Wiley, 1948).
[2] Buckley, Walter (Ed.), *Modern Systems Research for the Behavioral Scientist* (Chicago, Aldine, 1968).
[3] Emery, F. E. (Ed.), *Systems Thinking* (London, Penguin Books, 1969).

SOME CYBERNETIC THEORY

The starting point of cybernetics is the realisation that all control and communication systems, be they hardware and artificial or organic and naturally occurring, can be talked about from the point of view of control and communication in the same terms, and studied using the same set of concepts. This means that for cybernetic purposes the distinction between living and non-living is regarded as trivial. For this reason in cybernetics one tends to talk about 'systems'—a term which in itself is neutral with respect to the living/non-living dichotomy.

Let us look at some of the concepts that can be applied equally well to living and artificial systems. We can do this in terms of the three 'c's of cybernetics: control, communication and computation.

(1) *Control*

Among the most basic concepts in the study of control are the related ideas of homeostasis and negative feedback.

A system is said to be *homeostatic* if it is able to maintain certain of its variables within certain specifiable limits. For example, a pressure cooker maintains pressure within certain limits, not allowing it to go above or below these limits. Again, a thermostat maintains the temperature of a room within specifiable limits, not allowing it to become too hot or too cold. Similarly, the temperature of the blood in the human body is maintained within limits. As a final example, a man driving a car normally tries to keep the car on the road and as long as he does so we can say that the situation is homeostatic. Of these four examples, the first two refer to non-living systems, the third to a living system, and the fourth to a combined living (driver) and non-living (car) system.

Systems which are homeostatic are usually also *adaptive* systems: they adapt themselves in certain respects in order to maintain homeostasis in a changing environment. For example, the thermostat maintains the temperature of the room by adapting the amount of heat provided in such a way as to counteract the effects of fluctuations of heat in the environment (provided these are not too extreme). And the car driver adapts the orientation of the car to the changing direction of the road.

Negative feedback can be used by a system in the attempt to maintain homeostasis. By negative feedback is meant that some part of the output of the system is fed back into the system again in a negative direction in order to control that system. So if the output deviates from some required amount the output itself tends to drive the system back to producing the required output. This can be represented by the following diagram:

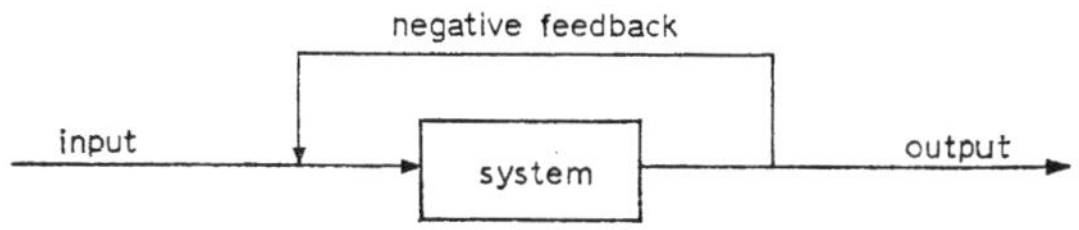

FIG. 1

We can understand the controlling effect of negative feedback if we examine how homeostasis is maintained in the examples just given.

The simplest form of pressure cooker is simply a saucepan with a lid. If water is boiled in this, sooner or later enough pressure of steam is built up to raise the lid of the saucepan. As soon as the lid is raised, however, the steam is let out and the pressure in the saucepan decreases rapidly until the lid falls back in place. But as soon as pressure is built up again, so the lid re-opens; and so on. What happens is that part of the output of the system, the pressure, controls the system so that the pressure itself maintains, through the lid, a level of pressure which fluctuates within certain limits.

With a thermostat, the heat in the room itself can be used to activate a switch which turns off the heating. The heating automatically recommences when the heat of the room is no longer sufficient to keep the switch turned off. ('Error-actuated' devices in engineering, of which there are many examples, are referred to as 'servo-mechanisms'.)

The control of blood temperature is much more complex, but briefly what happens is that when the temperature of the blood exceeds the normal temperature of 98·6°F neurons in the hypothalamus which are sensitive to temperature set into operation essentially negative feedback activity (evaporative cooling of the blood through perspiration and increased thermal radiation from the blood through expansion of blood vessels near the skin) which results in the blood temperature being lowered. The term 'homeostasis' was first used prominently in modern science by Walter B. Cannon, the great American physiologist, to refer to just this kind of process in the body and his classic book[1] contains a wide range of examples of physiological homeostasis.

[1] Cannon, Walter B., *The Wisdom of the Body* (New York, Norton, 1932).

In the case of the car driver keeping the car on the road, any movement (or lack of movement) by him of the steering wheel which causes the car to move away from its desired position on the road causes him to note that the position is no longer correct and to move the steering wheel in the opposite direction from the direction of error. That is, movement by the car away from the desired position results in action being taken which corrects the error. As in the other examples, error leads to error-compensation.

If the source of deviation in the output is to any significant extent outside the system, negative feedback may not be enough to overcome the resultant variation in the variables being controlled. For example, if the heat of a room becomes too low because it is snowing outside, it may not be possible to bring the room up to the required minimum temperature. But negative feedback will always be tending to drive the variables back *towards* their desired values.

A system may control its behaviour, using negative feedback, not only to attempt to maintain a state it is already in but to attempt to achieve some state it has not yet been in. For example, a car driver may act in such a way that he not only keeps his car on the road, but also so that he reaches his destination by a given time. This he may accomplish by reference to his watch and a map (or to subjective estimates of distance and time), speeding up whenever it appears that the desired end-state will not in fact be achieved. A missile homing on a moving target would be another example of this kind of purposeful system. In such cases some form of model or representation of the desired end-state is required with which the system can compare its present state in order to take the necessary (negative feedback) action to reduce the discrepancy.

Besides negative feedback, there is also the opposite process of positive feedback: in this case part of the output of the system is fed back into the system again in a positive direction in order to amplify rather than reduce deviations in the system. An example of positive feedback is the process of investment—the more money one has the more money one can make, the more money one has. However, positive feedback can be incorporated within a system in such a way as to increase the effectiveness of negative feedback. Power brakes exemplify this situation: here pressure on the brake, which is a form of negative feedback controlling the speed of the vehicle, is automatically amplified by means of a positive feedback arrangement.

(Actually, control theory is much more complicated than has

been implied so far and involves notions such as inertia, delay and oscillation. But we do not have the space here to discuss the theory in more detail.)

The importance of feedback mechanisms in both artificial and living systems was recognised by Wiener as early as the first years of the second world war when he was engaged on the problem of the prediction of flight of enemy aircraft by anti-aircraft gunners and the design of computing equipment (this was in the early days of modern computer development) to aid in this. He found that both the behaviour of the human gunners and of the computing devices could be described in feedback terms.

An important point concerning feedback was first made in 1943 in a paper by Wiener and two other researchers, Rosenblueth and Bigelow.[1] This was that there is nothing mysterious about purposeful behaviour, but that it can be a property of machines as well as living organisms. The centuries' old teleological argument of the vitalists, that an essential difference between men and machines is that the former are purposeful and the latter not, does not therefore seem to hold up. And the argument that purpose is not subject to the cause-and-effect laws of natural science because it involves action towards the future is also seen as not valid. Although in purposeful behaviour the future (in the form of some goal) seems to affect the present, such behaviour can in fact be analysed, as we have seen, entirely in cause-and-effect terms.

(2) *Communication*

It should be obvious that control cannot occur in any system without communication. A man driving a car cannot keep it on the road if (a) he receives no (visual) information from outside the car or (b) he cannot in effect transmit information through the steering wheel to the wheels of the car. Similarly a thermostat cannot function if it is completely insensitive to the changing heat in the room it is controlling or if it cannot in turn affect the amount of heat in the room. It is clear from these two examples that we can talk about the passage of information in control systems and that by this we mean something more general than the everyday use of the term information to refer to the content of speech and other deliberately communicative signals. In fact the notion of a message in cybernetics is one of the utmost generality and is even more fundamental than that of feedback and homeostasis.

[1] Rosenblueth, A., Wiener, N., and Bigelow, J., 'Behaviour, purpose and teleology', *Philosophy of Science* (1943), vol. 10, pp. 18–24.

In order to build control and communication systems and to understand the functioning of living control and communication systems it is necessary to be able to measure amounts of information in messages in a precise and quantitative way. It was in order to do this that *Information Theory* (or 'Communication Theory') was developed. In fact a number of theories of information have been suggested, but it is probably true to say that the formulation of Shannon[1] is the most widely accepted and used today. When we refer to Information Theory, then, we shall be referring to this theory. (The term 'cybernetics' is sometimes used, especially on the continent, as more or less synonymous with 'information theory'. It is true that information theory is one of the most central strands that go to make up cybernetics, but this difference of terminology represents one of the major differences of emphasis in the use of the term that was referred to earlier in the chapter.[2])

Information theory is a branch of probability theory. It can be used in situations involving sequences of events in which a probability value can be attached consistently to the occurrence of each event. When this can be done, the amount of information in a given event at a given moment can be estimated, as can the combined amount of information in a series of events. Thus if we take it that the probability of each face of a die is one sixth on each throw, we can measure the amount of information contained in a series of throws. Similarly if we have a probability estimate for the occurrence of each letter of the alphabet in English (frequency probabilities of this kind have been estimated by means of sampling procedures) we can work out on this basis the amount of information contained in a particular English message, e.g. in 'Trespassers will be prosecuted'. (Methods have also been developed which allow information theory to be used with continuous as well as discrete messages.)

The more random, and therefore unpredictable, a sequence of events or symbols constituting a message is, the more the information in the message. This may seem an odd way to think of information but there is a sense in which this idea is not inconsistent with our intuitive understanding of the meaning of 'information'. If I telephone my bookie to find out who won the 3.30 and he tells me that a given outsider won the race there will be more information in

[1] See Shannon, C. E., and Weaver, W., *The Mathematical Theory of Communication* (Urbana, University of Illinois Press, 1949).

[2] To confuse things even further the term 'information science' is sometimes used to refer to the field of computer engineering; and, as we have seen, the term 'information-processing models' is applied to computer models of behaviour.

this message than if he told me that the favourite won—as the latter is more probable or more to be expected. If I ask a friend what sort of weather he had on his holiday on the French Riviera in the summer and he tells me that it snowed there will be more information in his answer than if he tells me that the weather was fine. If I say to you, the reader, 'you are now reading this sentence' there is no information in the words in inverted commas since the probability of the words being correct is '1', i.e. there is no uncertainty. So information has an inverse relation to probability or expectancy on the part of the receiver of the message: the more probable the message, the less the information.

If information already present in a message is repeated, this inessential information is said to be *redundant*, and a measure is available for the amount of such redundancy in a message. Although redundancy increases the inefficiency of a communications system it can also increase its reliability: if information being transmitted is interfered with by 'noise', sufficient redundancy can overcome the effects of the noise.

Just like control theory, information theory can be used to refer to both living and non-living systems: the set of probabilistic events could be the letters of the English alphabet, the frequencies of English words when used in a given context, the alternative responses available to a subject in a psychology experiment, the 'coding' molecules of DNA, the different morse code signals, the notes of the piano, a set of numbers to be operated on by a computer, etc., etc.

It should be made clear, however, that information theory says nothing about the meaning of a message. So in information theory terms, where for example the probabilistic events are taken to be the letters of the English alphabet, the phrase 'Visitors are kindly requested not to feed the animals' would contain exactly the same amount of information as 'kindly animals are requested not to feed the visitors', or as 'are not kindly visitors to animals feed requested the', or even 'aerottonikdnylivissrotslaminaeefdqerseudetteh'.[1]

(3) *Computation*

Although the term 'computation' immediately brings to mind the idea of mathematical calculation, it can be used in a rather broader way to refer to the carrying out of any effective procedure. It will

[1] An excellent introduction, especially oriented to the needs of psychologists, is: Edwards, Elwyn, *Information Transmission* (London, Chapman and Hall, 1964). Also of special interest to psychologists is: Attneave, Fred, *Applications of Information Theory to Psychology* (New York, Holt, Rinehart and Winston, 1959).

be remembered from Chapter 1 that the term 'effective' is used to refer to procedures which are both complete and consistent. Many procedures other than those involved in mathematical calculation may be effective and therefore regarded as forms of computation. Thus computers may carry out mathematical computations, but they may also process information effectively in other ways and indeed most of the subsequent chapters of this book are about such computations.

Obviously the study of effective systems is central to cybernetics which is concerned with systems designed to achieve goals. The abstract study of effective procedures is called *automata theory*, an automaton being a certain kind of abstract logical or mathematical system embodying an effective procedure which it applies to inputs in order to find outputs. Unlike information theory, automata theory is concerned primarily with deterministic and not probabilistic systems, with what is possible under ideal conditions. An automaton is in fact rather like a diagram in geometry which represents abstract ideas (and in which the thickness of the lines can be disregarded).

Automata theory is concerned with what kinds of behaviour can and cannot in principle be achieved by different kinds of system: we could in fact call it the logic of systems. For example, what are the minimum properties which a system would need in order to carry out a computation of a particular kind? Or, is there any logical contradiction in the idea of a machine being able to reproduce itself, and if not, what are the requirements? (As far as the latter question is concerned, von Neumann[1] has demonstrated that machine self-reproduction *is* possible under certain conditions.[2])

Automata theory derives from that part of mathematics called *metamathematics* which is really part of philosophy. Metamathematics is not concerned with problems within mathematics or whether particular mathematical statements are true or false, but on the notion of proof itself: How do we know that statements in mathematics are true or false? What are the assumptions involved in this? How can we justify the rules of mathematics? Has mathematics been invented or discovered? In brief: what is mathematics?

Questions of this kind were very much stimulated in the present century by the publication of the *Principia Mathematica* of Russell

[1] von Neumann, J., 'The general and logical theory of automata', in *Cerebral Mechanisms in Behavior, the Hixon Symposium*, Ed. Jeffress, L. A. (New York, Wiley, 1951).

[2] Fortunately no one has yet let machines themselves into the secret.

and Whitehead.[1] They argued that mathematics is part of logic and can be reduced to it, and in order to facilitate their argument they invented modern symbolic logic. Two major forms of opposition to this 'logistic' viewpoint developed. One was the 'intuitionist' view of Brouwer[2] and others that mathematics does not have to be derived from anything else and that its basic concepts and modes of reference are to be found in intuition. The other, held especially by David Hilbert[3] the German mathematician, was the 'formalist' view that mathematics is nothing but marks on paper, symbols manipulated according to certain rules.[4]

If Hilbert's approach was correct it would be necessary to show that all of mathematics could be derived *mechanically* from the basic axioms and rules. That is, it would be necessary to show that there is an 'effective decision procedure' for the whole of mathematics. In fact, it has now been shown that the whole of classical mathematics does not have such a decision procedure, the best known proof of this being by Gödel.[5] But one approach to the problem was that of Alan Turing, the British mathematician, who suggested[6] that one might think in terms of theoretical machines (since called 'Turing machines') for carrying out mathematical computations.

Turing machines are theoretical automata. Although their original purpose was to carry out different mathematical computations, the conceptualisation of these machines is such a basic one that it is possible to ask whether a Turing machine could be produced to bring about any specifiable piece of behaviour. In other words, Turing machines are abstract systems by means of which it is possible to examine the logic of different processes. It would not be too much to say that the Turing machine idea, initially as a by-product of metamathematics, gave rise to the whole field of automata theory.

Although no one has ever bothered to construct a Turing mach-

[1] Russell, B., and Whitehead, A. N., *Principia Mathematica* (Cambridge University Press, 3 vols., 1910–13).
[2] Brouwer, L. E. J., 'Intuitionism and formalism', *Bull. Amer. Math. Soc.* (1913), **20**, 81–96.
[3] Hilbert, D., and Bernays, P., *Grundlagen der Mathematik* (Berlin, Springer, 2 vols., 1934, 1939).
[4] A clear exposition of all three points of view can be found in Kneebone, G. T., *Mathematical Logic and the Foundations of Mathematics* (New York, Van Nostrand, 1963).
[5] Gödel, K., 'Über formal unentscheidbare Sätze der Principia Mathematica und verwandter System 1', *Monatsh. Math. Phys.* (1931), **38**, 173–98.
[6] Turing, A. M., 'On computable numbers, with an application to the Entscheidungsproblem', *Proc. London Math. Soc.* (Second series 1936), **42**, 230–65.

ine (mainly because theoretical proofs are adequate), we could imagine that such a machine might appear as in the following diagram:

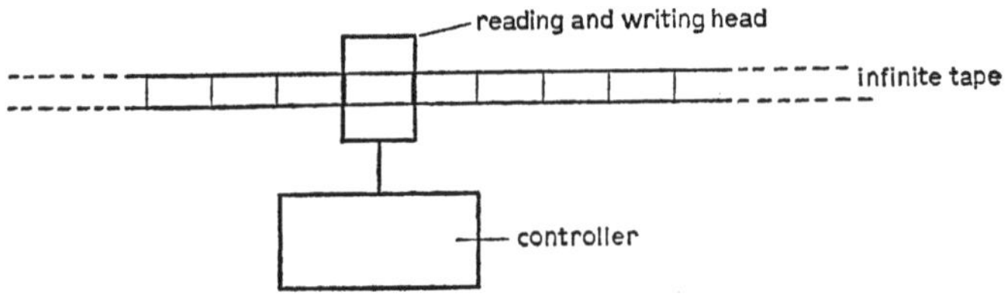

FIG. 2

As can be seen, it consists essentially of three parts: (i) an infinite linear tape divided into squares, each square carrying a symbol, (ii) a head which can read the symbol of whichever square lies on it at a given time, which can replace this symbol by another, and which can move the tape to the left or right, and (iii) a controller which contains the program for the machine and which controls the actions of the head in accordance with the program. The controller can be in any one of a finite number of different internal states.

The action of the machine at a given time depends on the conjunction of the symbol being read by the head at that time and the internal state of the controller at that time. For example, if the symbol '1' is being read and the machine is in state (3), the instruction in the program for this conjunction might be: 'Replace the symbol "1" by the symbol "0", move the tape one place to the left, and go into state (5).' Now that the machine is in state (5), the next symbol read might be another '1'. This time the relevant instruction might be: 'Leave the symbol "1" on the tape, move the tape one place to the left, and go to state (1).' For a Turing machine program to be effective there will normally have to be an instruction for every possible conjunction of internal state and symbol.

If the program for a Turing machine is in fact successful in that the machine inevitably accomplishes the purpose for which it was written, then the program may be said to be *algorithmic*. The term algorithm is in fact a general one which refers not only to Turing machine programs but to any unambiguously stated 'machine-like' procedure which, if followed literally, will inevitably achieve the intended result. In other words it is a synonym for 'effective procedure'. In these terms, automata theory is concerned with discovering whether there are algorithms for achieving different specifiable ends. And one way of determining this is by trying to write a program for a Turing machine to achieve this end.

There is another major class of automata used in automata theory; this is the class of *networks* of different kinds which transform sets of inputs in various spatial and temporal configurations into sets of outputs of different spatial and temporal configurations. The classic work here is that of McCulloch and Pitts.[1] A network consists of a set of elements interconnected in a spatial pattern which governs which elements fire into which other elements and whether the result of firing into another element is in each case excitatory or inhibitory. If Turing machines are sometimes called 'infinite automata' because of the tapes of infinite length which they use, networks are called 'finite automata'. Another difference between the two kinds of automata is that the algorithm of a given network is implicit in its structure rather than being contained explicitly in a set of instructions as it is with a Turing machine. However, networks can be represented by sets of formulae in symbolic logic (hence 'logical nets' as they are sometimes called). So if infinite automata take their inspiration from the formalist approach to metamathematics, finite automata derive more from the logistic approach.

We saw when considering control theory and communication theory that both theories can be used to refer to both living and non-living systems. The same is true of automata theory. Thus Turing showed it would be possible to have a Turing machine (called a 'Universal Turing machine') which could carry out any of the computations which could be carried out by any other Turing machine, i.e. which would accept any of the programs of any other Turing machines. This demonstration of the logical viability of a general purpose Turing machine encouraged the development in hardware of a general purpose computation machine: the digital computer. Turing also demonstrated that a Universal Turing machine does not need a complete description of another Turing machine whose computation it is to carry out but that a suitably written 'short code' will suffice. This underlies the use of autocodes (to be described in Chapter 3) in digital computers. At the same time, Turing machines have been used to refer to living systems by modelling biological processes like development[2] and enzyme

[1] McCulloch, W. S., and Pitts, W., 'A logical calculus of the ideas immanent in nervous activity', *Bull. Math. Biophys.* (1943), **5**, 115–33.

[2] Apter, M. J., *Cybernetics and Development* (Oxford, Pergamon, 1966).

systems.[1] Similarly computers function essentially by means of networks of elements inter-connected in various ways, while networks are also used to simulate functioning of the nervous system, each element representing a neuron.[2, 3]

ABSTRACT TO CONCRETE

As will by now have been realised, cybernetics cannot be dismissed as involving no more than the simple drawing of analogies between various machine and living systems: from the cybernetic point of view certain organisational features of both machines and organisms may be regarded as *identical* at the more abstract level of control theory, information theory and automata theory. Thus from the cybernetic point of view the brain is not just like a computer, but in some of its aspects may be identical in function with a computer programmed in certain ways.

It is possible to argue[4] that one important feature of this situation from the point of view of the biological sciences, including psychology, is that it gives them the chance to achieve the same kind of generality as physics and chemistry. That is to say, through cybernetics the biological sciences need no longer be restricted to *actual* systems but can consider *possible* systems as well—in the same way that, for example, a physicist can talk about perfect gases or a chemist can create synthetic substances that do not occur naturally.

The theory of cybernetics should help both in building more sophisticated machinery and in understanding living processes. At the same time, the stimulus of practical needs for machinery to perform certain tasks and the stimulus of trying to understand various complicated biological and psychological processes should both help in the further development of theory.

If we regard cybernetics as possessing three poles of interest, living, non-living and abstract systems, we have seen how abstract systems relate to the other two. At the same time, the other two have a more direct relationship in cybernetics: it is possible to study and construct hardware machines (and write computer programs) in order to gain an increased understanding of the way in which living

[1] Stahl, W. R., and Goheen, H. E., 'Molecular algorithms', *J. Theoret. Biol.* (1963), **5**, 2, 266–87.
[2] McCulloch and Pitts, op. cit.
[3] George, F. H., *Automation, Cybernetics and Society* (London, Hill, 1959), ch. 13.
[4] As I have done in more detail in Apter (1966), op. cit., ch. 1.

systems function, and conversely to study living systems in order to gain ideas as to how more sophisticated—and by this is meant more adaptive, flexible, intelligent, self-organising and life-like—machines could be built. (The latter approach to engineering is sometimes referred to as 'Bionics'.[1]) In some cases, of course, both aims are pursued concurrently where a given process in living systems is studied parallel to the construction of a machine to achieve the same ends (e.g. perception, learning, etc.). Also it is probably true to say that even in research which involves a direct comparison of living and non-living processes reference is made to the more abstract level of cybernetics.

We can picture the structure of cybernetics, then, in the following way:

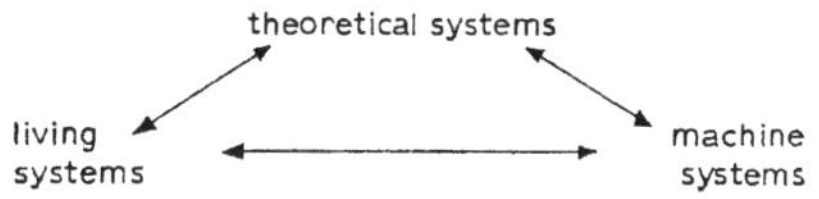

FIG. 3

We have looked at the theoretical level of cybernetics. Let us now therefore look briefly at cybernetic research aimed more directly at either understanding organisms or having practical application.

As we have seen, when it comes to trying to understand organismic functions, a standard cybernetic technique is to design or construct models invested with the same functions. There are three main classes of such models: (i) paper-and-pencil models, (ii) computer models, and (iii) hardware models. We have already mentioned some paper-and-pencil models (e.g. networks which learn, and Turing machine models of enzyme processes). The rest of this book is devoted to the topic of computer models. Let us here just glance at one example of a hardware model.

One of the best-known models in the whole of cybernetics must be the 'mechanical tortoise' model of Grey Walter.[2] This model demonstrates how life-like purposeful behaviour can be produced by a comparatively simple mechanism: the mechanism of scanning. The model, which he calls in a mock scientific way 'Machina Speculatrix', does indeed look something like a tortoise, since the machin-

[1] See: Gérardin, Lucien, *Bionics* (London, Weidenfeld and Nicolson, World University Library, 1968).

[2] Walter, W. Grey, *The Living Brain* (London, Duckworth, 1953).

ery is hidden by a protective shell; all that emerges are a tricycle undercarriage, which is driven by an electric motor, and a 'head' consisting of a photo-electric cell which rotates and scans the environment. This cell is connected to the front wheel so that the tortoise moves in whatever direction the cell is pointing. When an adequate source of light impinges on the cell it stops rotating and hence the machine heads towards the light. The tortoise also contains another sensory mechanism, but one of a 'tactile' rather than 'visual' character. The shell of the tortoise hangs loosely around the animal, so that if it touches something the shell is pushed in and makes an electrical contact. This causes the photo-cell of the head to work like an oscillator instead of scanning, so that the tortoise now alternately advances briefly and retreats and goes on doing so until it gets around the object, which it eventually does.

Despite the simplicity of this device, it behaves in a strikingly life-like manner. Placed in a room it searches until it finds an adequate light source, struggling around objects in order to get there. The situation may be made more life-like by bringing into the room a certain small container with a strong light above it which the tortoise is therefore attracted to enter: inside this container the tortoise's batteries are automatically recharged. Finally, even more manifestly purposeful behaviour is demonstrated in later more complex forms of the model which incorporate learning circuits.

As far as practical applications of cybernetics are concerned the central field is that which is referred to by the term *artificial intelligence*. Workers in this field are attempting to produce systems, especially computer systems, of ever-increasing intelligence and independence for everyday use in factories, schools and elsewhere. How much this work has so far contributed of real and immediate practical importance is arguable, but its potential in the long-term must be enormous. To give an example: a computer system which could understand natural language in both spoken and handwritten form and communicate in natural language would have considerable advantage in practical situations over one of the present generation of computers and computer programs.

Obviously the development of a language-using computer would be closely bound up with studies of the computer simulation of language behaviour in humans, and in general many research projects in artificial intelligence could be classified equally well as research projects in computer simulation. So the *synthesis* of artificial intelligence and the *simulation* of human intelligence to some extent overlap, and we shall therefore be looking at some of the field of artificial intelligence in the remaining chapters of this book. Indeed, if it were not for the field of artificial intelligence, the number of programs which could be interpreted in the light of computer simulation would be much depleted.

The aim of applying cybernetics to industry is to go further than automation by extending even further the range of autonomy of industrial equipment. For example, one could envisage equipment which not only controlled itself but also repaired itself when it went wrong; one could envisage equipment which could learn for itself how best to carry out various ill-defined tasks; and one could even envisage automating many managerial processes including much of the decision-making that takes place in the board room. The term *cybernation* is sometimes used to refer to aims of this kind to go further than automation. Although the successful attainment of such aims undoubtedly lies in the distant future, work has already started with such long-term aims in view.

In education, the field of *computer assisted instruction* is developing rapidly. Not only are experiments being made into using computers to teach children, but in some parts of the United States computers are already being used regularly in the classroom. The technique of 'time-sharing' (see Chapter 3) allows a large number of students to use the computer simultaneously, each student having his own terminal to the computer, consisting, for example, of a typewriter/paper-tape punch for computer input and a cathode-ray tube display for computer output. Specially written programs allow the computer to interact with each student it is teaching in much the same manner as a human tutor might interact with a student: presenting information, asking questions, and then presenting more information adapted to the needs of the student as demonstrated by his success or lack of success in answering the questions. In some cases the student can also ask the computer questions.[1]

It will now be appreciated that cybernetics is in a sense more an attitude than a strict subject-matter: an attitude characterised by a passion for precision and a contempt for ideas that cannot be expressed in effective form, a desire to search for common organisational features in purposeful systems superficially unlike one another, a feeling that organisms are essentially constructible, and a belief that it will be possible to create future generations of machin-

[1] A simple introduction to this part of the field of artificial intelligence is given in Apter, M. J., *The New Technology of Education* (London, Macmillan, 1968), ch. 4.

ery that will be more independent from and intellectually successful than their creators. This attitude has in turn stimulated the emergence of a host of sophisticated concepts and practical techniques.

The computer simulation of behaviour can be regarded as one of the expressions of the cybernetic attitude and is indeed closely bound up with the whole development of cybernetics. It constitutes much more than the far-fetched and irrelevant analogy which some people have claimed it is, being related as we have seen to the rigorous fields of control theory, information theory and automata theory and to the practical field of artificial intelligence.

SELECTED REFERENCES

Ashby, W. Ross., *An Introduction to Cybernetics* (London, Chapman and Hall, 1956).

Beer, Stafford, *Cybernetics and Management* (London, English Universities Press, 1959).

George, F. H., *Cybernetics and Biology* (Edinburgh, Oliver and Boyd, 1965).

Guilbaud, G. T., *What is Cybernetics?* (London, Heinemann, 1959).

Klir, J., and Valach, M., *Cybernetic Modelling* (London, Iliffe, 1967).

Pask, Gordon, *An Approach to Cybernetics* (London, Hutchinson, 1961).

Rose, J. (Ed.), *Survey of Cybernetics* (London, Iliffe, 1970).

Singh, Jagjit, *Great Ideas in Information Theory, Language and Cybernetics* (New York, Dover Publications, 1966).

Wiener, Norbert, *Cybernetics* (New York, Wiley, 1948).

Wiener, Norbert, *The Human Use of Human Beings* (London, Eyre and Spottiswoode, 1954).

3

DIGITAL COMPUTING

A BRIEF HISTORY OF COMPUTERS

Digital computers have burst into public awareness so recently that it is sometimes difficult to realise that they have any history or antecedents at all. Yet if we were to regard the *abacus* as a primitive computer we could say that the history of computers goes back thousands of years before Christ.

However, the first device that one could perhaps call a machine for calculating was the adding machine devised by *Blaise Pascal* in 1642 (when he was aged only nineteen). This consisted of a set of cogs each of which could be turned by anything from one tenth to nine tenths of a turn and connected in such a way that the complete turn of one cog would automatically move the adjacent cog by one tenth of a turn—this representing, for example, $9+1=10$. In this way adding and subtracting were mechanised.

Leibnitz's multiplication machine (1671) represents the next development. This made use of the fact that multiplication is simply repeated addition, and was able to perform such repeated addition automatically. He thus created essentially the modern calculating machine.

The next step towards the computer did not occur until the early nineteenth century when *Charles Babbage*, the famous British eccentric, conceived of his 'Difference engine'. This was designed to calculate automatically certain mathematical tables, e.g. tables of squares, and also to print them out once they were calculated. The construction of the machine was sponsored by the British government, but for various reasons only a small part of it was actually built.

Babbage also designed another machine which he called the 'Analytic engine' which was intended to be more general in purpose and even more automatic in function than the Difference engine. It was to have been controlled by punched cards similar to those which had recently been introduced by *Jacquard* to control weaving machines. In the Jacquard machines, use of a control card allowed the weaving machine to alternate colours of the yarn in a way specified by the program on the card so that complex patterns could be built up by the machine automatically, i.e. without human interference. Different patterns could be produced by the simple expedient of putting different cards in the machine. In a similar way Babbage hoped to make the sequence of actions required in a calculation entirely dependent on a punched card program and to be able to carry out a variety of kinds of calculations by changing the cards. Although the simple mechanisms envisaged by Babbage for realising the computations are a far cry from the electronics of modern computers, Babbage's machine was in conception essentially the same as the modern general purpose computer and if anyone deserves the honour of being called the inventor of the computer it must be Babbage. Unfortunately, the machine was never built and his ideas lay dormant for nearly a hundred years.

The idea of using punched cards for automatic information processing was, however, taken up late in the nineteenth century by *Hermann Hollerith*, who was faced with the problem of tabulating the enormous amount of data accumulated in the United States census in 1890. He decided to use punched cards to represent the information to be tabulated (not the program as in Babbage's machine) so that the information could be processed, at least in part, automatically. Each card represented an individual and was divided into 240 squares. A hole in a given square had a particular meaning, e.g. that the individual was aged between forty and forty-five years. Each card representing each individual was placed in the tabulating machine in turn and all the information in it relayed automatically to dials which kept a running total of each characteristic, e.g. the numbers of people in different age groups. Since that time the use of punched cards, especially in accounting, has become widespread.

The beginning of the most recent stage in the history of the development of the digital computer dates from 1937 when *Howard H. Aiken* of Harvard University started to build, in co-operation with International Business Machines Inc., the so-called 'Mark I' computer which was completed in 1944. This constituted the realisation for the first time of a calculating machine which was general purpose (i.e. could carry out a wide range of different programs like a Jacquard weaving machine) and automatic in operation. Information was inserted by means of punched paper tape. It was in fact the first general purpose digital computer ever built. But in operation it was not electronic but electromechanical, and used moving parts.

The first *electronic* computer built was the ENIAC (Electronic Numerical Integrator and Calculator) at the University of Pennsylvania in 1946. It had no moving parts and used valves in its electronic circuits.

Another computer of historical importance was the EDVAC (Electronic Discrete Variable Automatic Calculator) with which the name of John von Neumann is usually associated. This machine used the binary system (see p. 54) for the first time and was also the first to store the operating instructions internally.

In the development of the modern general purpose electronic digital computer we can discern a number of trends which have continued up to the present and appear likely to continue in the future:

(1) The first is the increase in *generality* of the computer. Babbage's Difference engine could only compute certain mathematical tables whereas a modern general purpose computer can in principle carry out any calculation which can be done by any other machine, provided its storage space is large enough. This possibility was in fact proved, even before Aiken's Mark I computer was built, by A. M. Turing (see Chapter 2). A modern computer can even do things which some people may not regard as calculations at all, including not only information retrieval and business data processing[1] but also playing games, using language, and so on. Most of this book is in fact about such computer functioning. The term 'computer' is nowadays possibly too restricting since it implies in everyday terms that the device is confined to mathematical calculation. For this reason it might be better, if the term 'general purpose computer' had not

[1] For example, the computer might store all the names of the customers of the company together with information about them. It could then be programmed to select ('retrieve') on demand the names of customers, e.g. who have previously bought a certain type of item, who owe more than a certain amount of money, or who have orders outstanding.

already become so widely established, to use instead some such term as 'general purpose symbol manipulator', or 'general purpose information processor'.

It is this very generality of the computer which so many people find difficult to grasp. Most machines, like cars and refrigerators and cricket bats, are for doing something fairly specific, and are understood in terms of what they do. The computer, by contrast, is a machine which can behave in an extremely large number of ways—as many ways as there are programs which can be written for it. Just as the rules of grammar together with the finite set of words available in a language can generate an unlimited number of sentences, so the programs which can be written for a computer are relatively unlimited, although restricted eventually by considerations like the size of the memory store.

(2) A second trend is the increase in *autonomy* of the computer. With the calculating machines of Pascal and Leibnitz the human operator was needed to interact with the machine continually, putting in each new number at the moment it was required during the calculation and noting down intermediate results. With a modern computer there is normally no need for the operator to do anything at all during the computation after he has entered the program and data and pressed a start button.

Another step leading to greater independence of the computer from the human element was the development of *autocodes* which allow the programmer to write programs in stylised forms of English rather than in terms of the sets of numbers which, as we shall see, must be fed into the computer storage to represent the program. This not only makes it considerably more convenient to write programs for the computer, but also the program which the computer uses to translate the autocode program into a form usable by the computer usually also determines which parts of the storage of the computer are to be used in different parts of the calculation, and hence increases computer autonomy.

The next step towards computer autonomy will be to use techniques which allow the computer to write the details of a program for itself, the programmer simply specifying the aims of the program. This is one of the objects of research in 'heuristic' programming techniques which we shall look at in Chapter 5.

(3) The *increase in speed* of functioning of digital computers represents one of the most startling aspects of computer technology. While one would probably have measured the speed of functioning of Babbage's Difference engine in seconds, the speed of the first

generation of modern computers using vacuum tubes and valves could be measured in milliseconds (10^{-3}). The speed of the next generation using transistors could be measured in microseconds (10^{-6}) and of the most recent generation, using solid state techniques, in nanoseconds (10^{-9}).[1]

(4) Another notable trend in the development of computers has been the *decrease in size* which has occurred. It has been estimated that Aiken's Mark I computer was only about one tenth of the size Babbage's Analytical engine would have been if built.[2] Since then, computer size has decreased still further. Sir Leon Bagrit has expressed this in the following way: '. . . whereas the computer of 1950 needed a large room to contain it, the 1964 model is down to the dimensions of a suitcase: by 1974 the normal computer will be no bigger than a packet of a hundred cigarettes.'[3] Concomitant with the decrease in size has been a decrease in cost for a computer of a given capability.

In this section the development of *digital* computers has been traced. There is, however, another type of computer: the *analogue* computer. If the digital computer is a sophisticated calculating machine, the analogue computer is a sophisticated slide-rule. The distinction is the same as that between counting and measuring, between dealing with discrete symbols and manipulating continuous physical quantities. With analogue computers, physical quantities—usually of an electrical nature (like the voltage between two points in a circuit)—are used to represent variables in the calculation concerned, i.e. variables have physical *analogues*. The modern analogue computer antedates the modern digital computer and analogue computers of various kinds have been used widely by engineers since the 1920s, especially that type of analogue computer called a *differential analyser* used to work out, as the name implies, differential equations. However, the analogue computer is considerably restricted in comparison with the general purpose digital computer in that a given analogue computer can only carry out certain kinds of calculations: that is, analogue computers are all, more or less, special purpose. Their significance, certainly in the

[1] It is not intended to go into any of the details of computer hardware in this book. Some of the books recommended at the end of this chapter should be referred to by the reader interested in this aspect of computers.

[2] Borko, Harold (Ed.), *Computer Applications in the Behavioral Sciences* (New Jersey, Prentice-Hall, 1962), p. 42.

[3] Bagrit, Sir Leon, *The Age of Automation* (The Reith Lectures 1964, London, Penguin Books, 1966), p. 33.

field we are studying in this book, is much less at the present time than that of the digital computer, and analogue simulations of behaviour are comparatively rare in contrast to the large numbers of behavioural simulation programmes that have now been written for the digital computer. The analogue computer, therefore, will not be dealt with in any more detail here.

HOW A DIGITAL COMPUTER WORKS

In this section and the next a certain amount of detail is given concerning computers and programming. This may not seem to be of immediate interest to psychologists, but it is essential reading if the mystery is to be taken out of computers and the argument in later chapters is to be understood.

Let us then look first at the overall structure and mode of functioning of a modern general purpose digital computer. The structure of a computer can be represented by the following diagram:

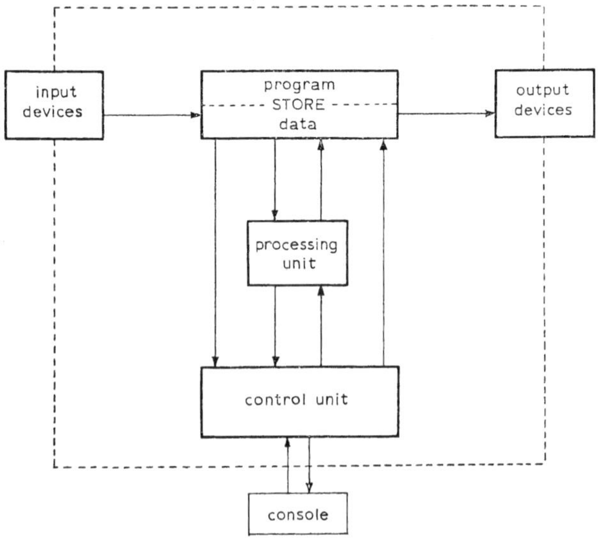

FIG. 4

A digital computer consists of four main parts: a part to read information in and out of the computer, a part for storing information in the computer, a part for actually carrying out computations, and a part for controlling the computer. Let us consider each of these parts in turn.

(1) *Input and output devices*

By input and output devices are meant devices for translating information into a form which can be manipulated by the computer and entering it, and for translating information back out again into a form which the computer user can utilise and making it accessible to him.

There are two kinds of information which must be entered into the computer in order for it to carry out a computation: the *program*, or instructions for carrying out the computation, and *data* for the program to work on. For example, if one wants to work out whether various sets of results from experiments have means which are significantly different from each other, one needs a program to test for significant differences between means, and also the data, or results generated in the experiments, for the program to work on.

Sometimes programs are 'pre-wired' in the computer which means that only data needs to be entered into the computer. More usually both data and program are put into the computer, and the same methods are used for entering both. One of the most widely adopted methods is to use paper tape punched by means of a teleprinter. Paper tape can also be used for the computer output, the information being coverted into printed output by means of the reading unit of the teleprinter. Punched cards are also often used for input and output. And there is frequently a facility for entering information directly into the computer by means of an electric typewriter connected to the computer.

More recently, graphical devices have been developed for the computer display of information, especially in the form of cathode-ray tubes (CRTs).

(2) *Memory store*

As we have seen, the store holds both the program and the data for the program to work on. In some computers they are held in different parts of the store, in others either program or data information can be contained in any part of the store. Numbers generated during a computation are also stored.

The program is represented in the store as a series of numbers and in this sense is indistinguishable from the data. However, the computer operator starts the computer operating at a given point in the store where the program numbers start and it obeys these instructions sequentially until it reaches the instruction numbers which represent the instruction to stop. For the program writer, as we shall see, each computer has a dictionary for translating instructions into numbers. A program may then be written, translated into the appropriate numbers, and entered into the computer.

All information, both program and data, is normally represented in the computer by devices which have two possible states; for example, the presence or absence of an electrical pulse. (The input-output system also represents information in terms of two states: usually the presence or absence of a hole in a particular square of the punched tape or card.) So arithmetic is performed in the computer using the *binary scale* rather than the decimal scale which is the conventional scale which we learn to use in everyday life.

In the binary scale there are, as the name implies, only two symbols instead of the ten symbols of the decimal scale. The two symbols are '0' and '1'. ('0' can be represented by the absence of a pulse, '1' by the presence of a pulse.) Exactly the same rules of arithmetic are used with the binary as with the decimal scale. For example, just as with the decimal scale, in counting we add one extra digit every time we 'run out' of symbols. This will be clearer if we look at the binary representation of decimal numbers:

0	0
1	1
2	10
3	11
4	100
5	101
6	110
7	111
8	1000
9	1001
10	1010
11	1011 etc.

The store itself is divided effectively into small 'cells' each of which can contain up to a certain amount of information. These cells are called *locations* and each location has an *address*, i.e. a number which describes where it is in the computer. The information in such a location is called a computer *word*. The program, as we shall see, normally manipulates data by referring to the locations containing the data rather than by referring to the data directly.

A given computer word in a given location will be either a number or an instruction.

Computer stores differ in capacity in both the size of their locations, i.e. the length of the words which can be stored in them, and in the number of locations available. They also differ in their speed of access to information. In general, the greater the capacity the lower the speed of access and *vice versa.* To help get over this problem, computers stores are usually in two parts: (i) an immediate store which is comparatively small and high speed and (ii) a backing store which, although it is comparatively slow, has a large capacity. Information which is used continually is placed in the immediate store, and information which is used less often is placed in the backing store.

(3) *Processing unit*

This is the part of the computer which actually performs the computation, i.e. which carries out the processes of addition, substraction, multiplication and division.

This unit is sometimes called the *arithmetic unit* although it can also carry out essentially *logical* operations like determining whether one number is larger than another, whether it is positive or negative, and whether it is equal to zero or not. These logical operations are especially important for decision making within a program: for example, which subsequent steps to be taken could be made to depend on whether the result of a particular calculation is negative or positive. Another device which is often used where the same calculation has to be repeated many times is, as we shall see, to set a number in storage at the number of repetitions required, to program the computer to subtract one from this number at the end of each calculation, and to stop (or branch to another part of the program) when this 'counter' number reaches zero.

(4) *Control unit*

The control unit, as its name implies, directs the activity of the arithmetic unit. It does so in conformity with the program in the memory store and, when the occasion arises, in conjunction with information generated by the program, such as that leading to a branch decision in the example just given. (See Fig. 4 for the structure of a computer.)

The control unit also moves information from the memory store to the processing unit and back again as and when it is required and controls the timing of all operations.

The control console of a computer gives the computer operator direct access to the control unit and through it to the rest of the computer. It is used to start and stop the computer, to warn the operator when malfunctioning occurs, and to allow direct manual operation of the computer should this be required. It may also be used to clear the store, i.e. to delete everything in the store so that a new program and new data can be entered.

One recent development in computer technology should be noted here. Input-output equipment is pathetically slow in comparison with the processing unit. What is the point of having a system which can carry out a computation in a fraction of a second when it takes many seconds, or even minutes, to print out the result? Not only does the extra cost of such high-speed equipment seem unnecessary, but once there it is not made full use of because it stands idle while the input-output equipment is functioning. One way of making full use of the speed of the computer is to have a number of people using it at the same time through individual input-output devices: that is, to have the computer working on a number of programs together, obeying instructions from each program in rotation. To each user the increase in time is negligible in comparison with the speed of input-output, and therefore to each user it appears as if he and he alone is using the computer. This new method reduces the effective cost of a computer because the cost is shared among a number of users, and because it ensures that computer time is not wasted. The term *time-sharing* is used to refer to this method, and computer systems with a set of input-output modules connected to the central processing unit for time-sharing are called *multiple-access* systems. For such a system to work, an *executive program* is necessary which organises the other programs in the computer so that they can be worked on 'at the same time'. Time-sharing is obviously a method which is going to be used widely in future, and is already being adopted rapidly.

COMPUTER PROGRAMMING

Having glanced briefly at the structure of the hardware of computers, we can now turn our attention to what has become called the 'software' of computers: computer programming and programming techniques.

To write a program for a computer one writes a list of instructions. Each instruction consists of two parts. The first part refers to an operation to be carried out (e.g. add) and is written in coded form as a number. The second refers to an address or addresses in the computer which contain the data which the operation is to act on or into which the resulting information is to be placed.

There are in the main two kinds of computers: those which accept programs written in a 'single-address' style, and those which accept programs written in 'triple-address' style.

With the *single-address* style, as the name implies, an instruction contains a number representing an operation and the address of a *single* location. What the computer does is to carry out the operation on the contents of the location specified and where relevant at the same time to the contents of what is called the *accumulator*. (The accumulator is in effect a special location.)

So if we wanted to add the content of location 197 (say '5') to the content of location 215 (say '12'), we should need three instructions: the first to place the contents of location 197 in the accumulator (i.e. place '5' in the accumulator), the second to add the contents of location 215 to the accumulator (giving '17' in the accumulator) and the third to place the sum in a previously empty location (e.g. place '17' in location 216). The instructions to do this might look like this:

7/197
1/215
8/216

where '7' means place in the accumulator, '1' means add, and '8' means place the result in the location specified.

The *triple-address* system is simpler from the programming point of view. Three locations are specified in an instruction: the two that are to be operated on, and the location that the result is to be placed in. For example, to do the same thing that was done in the single-address example just given, only one instruction would be needed

1/197/215/216

where, as before, '1' means add.

Let us now imagine that we have a simple computer of the triple-address variety which uses the following code to refer to some of its operations (it will have many other operations besides these):

Add	1
Subtract	2
Multiply	3
Divide	4

Suppose now that the following calculation is to be performed:

$$\frac{5(4+6)}{19-9}$$

Let us look at a program which would perform this elementary calculation and examine what happens in each of the relevant locations at each stage. We can imagine that the numbers to be operated on are ready in the store in the locations shown in the first row of the table.

Program	*Effect*	*Computer locations (after instructions effected)* 1	2	3	4	5	6	7
	(Numbers placed in store)	5	4	6	19	9		
1/2/3/6	4 is added to 6 and the result is placed in location 6	5	4	6	19	9	10	
3/6/1/6	10 is multiplied by 5 and the result replaces the previous number in location 6	5	4	6	19	9	50	
2/4/5/7	9 is subracted from 19 and the result placed in location 7	5	4	6	19	9	50	10
4/6/7/7	50 is divided by 10 and the result replaces the previous number in location 7	5	4	6	19	9	50	5

We should of course need to add to these instructions coded instructions to print out the content of location 7 and to stop.

Several things should be noticed about this program. First, the numbers in store are not deleted unless written over by new numbers: instead copies of them are used in the calculations. (But computers also of course have facilities for number deletion if required.) Secondly, numbers generated in the course of the calculation are stored as well. Remember, too, that the program does not refer directly to data, but refers to the addresses of the locations which contain it.

It might seem as extravagent to use a computer to work out this calculation as it would be to use a tape punch to manufacture confetti. Obviously one would normally only use a computer for calculations far more complex than this simple example which is given to convey the idea of how a computer works. But even with a trivial calculation it can be worth using a computer if the calculation has to be repeated many thousands of times. Suppose then, that calculations of the form of the example had to be repeated 1000 times, with 1000 different sets of numbers. The program to do this, i.e. to work out

$$\frac{a(b+c)}{d-e}$$

n number of times, is hardly more difficult to write and certainly no more difficult to run on a computer than it would be for the calculation to be done once only.

It would have exactly the same form as the previous calculation except that we should add a *branch* instruction at the end of the calculation to be used in conjunction with a *counter*. If examination of the counter by the computer showed that there were more sets of numbers to be calculated, the computer would return to the beginning of the calculation and repeat it with the next set of numbers. In other words, we set up a situation where the computer *loops* round and round the program until all the sets of figures have been calculated. The whole program including the branch instructions can be represented by means of the diagram in Fig 5.

But how, in actually writing the program, can we arrange for the computer to compute different values of the sets of variables each time through the loop? This can be done by means of instructions in the program which refer not to data but to the program itself: that is, the program has to be partially self-referential. What happens is that, at the end of the loop, instructions are provided which change the addresses throughout the program so that they now refer to new sets of numbers. For example, if we had, as suggested, 1000 different sets of values of the variables in the formula and we wished to calculate all of these so that we finished up with 1000 results, we could arrange things in the following way. (Many other ways of organising the program could also be devised.) We enter all the figures in the order *a, b, c, d, e,* over and over again until we have entered all one thousand sets of figures sequentially into the computer. If each figure goes in one location we shall need 5000 locations in the store for this. We shall also need 1000 locations

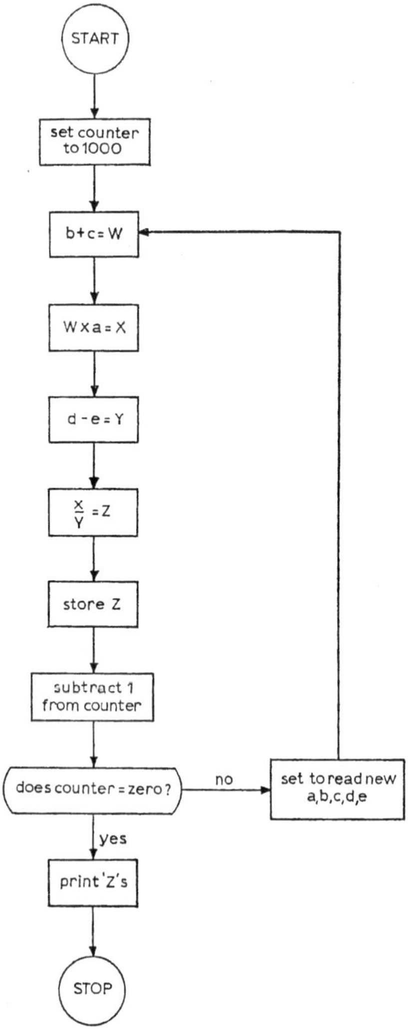
START
set counter to 1000
b+c=W
W x a=X
d-e=Y
$\frac{X}{Y}$ =Z
store Z
subtract 1 from counter
does counter = zero?
no
set to read new a,b,c,d,e
yes
print 'Z's
STOP

FIG. 5

to store all the answers, and 2 locations for use in working out each set of figures, as in the example above with a particular set of figures. (More than two locations will not be needed since the figures in these locations each time round the loop do not need to be retained if the result each time is stored elsewhere.) The relevant part of the program might now read as follows:

1/1002/1003/8000
3/8000/1001/8000
2/1004/1005/8001
4/8000/8001/8001

Here locations 8000 and 8001, well out of the way of the storage needed for the other numbers (arbitrarily placed in locations 1001 onwards), are used for the computer workings.

We should also need an instruction to the effect that the contents of 8001 are rewritten in e.g. location 9001.

Then, before starting the calculation again, the program adds 5 to all the addresses in the program except 8000 and 8001 and except the result storage addresses (which start at 9001) to which 1 is added. Then next time through the loop the *b* in 1007 is added to the *c* in 1008 etc., and the result of the whole calculation for that set of figures is placed in 9002. This kind of process is possible because, as we have seen, instructions are stored, coded in numerical form, just like data. Finally, when all 1000 calculations have been carried out, the results (in locations 9001 to 10,000) are printed out.

Fortunately, much of this housekeeping is nowadays looked after by the computer itself when autocodes are used. That is, the programmer instructs the computer in the autocode instructions to loop (if certain branching conditions are fulfilled) and the computer itself works out how to arrange the information in the locations in storage to allow this to occur. The ability to repeat a sub-set of instructions in a program as many times as are required, each time on different numbers (up to the limits of storage capacity), and to make certain modifications each time through, is one of the most powerful attributes of the modern computer.

What happens when an autocode is to be used is that a special program is fed into the computer which can translate any program written in the stylised but natural language of the autocode into the number language of the computer itself. Then the particular program in autocode is entered into the computer. There are several types of these translation programs and they go by different names. An *assembler* is the most rudimentary kind, and this is the type of translation program used with autocodes which closely resemble machine code (i.e. the number code of the computer) in the sense that each instruction in the autocode is translated into a single computer word. *Compilers* and *interpreters* are more sophisticated in that the autocodes used with these can have single instructions which represent strings of computer words, e.g. the instructions to go through the loop of a program again with different numbers which might be represented in autocode by one word but requires a number of machine instructions. The difference between a compiler and an interpreter is that the product of a compiler is a complete machine code program whereas an interpreter translates each statement as it is to be used by the computer. (This is rather like the difference between a human language translator and a conference interpreter.) The interpreter is usually uneconomic in terms of computer time, but may be convenient to the programmer in certain circumstances. With an assembler or compiler the situation can be depicted as follows:

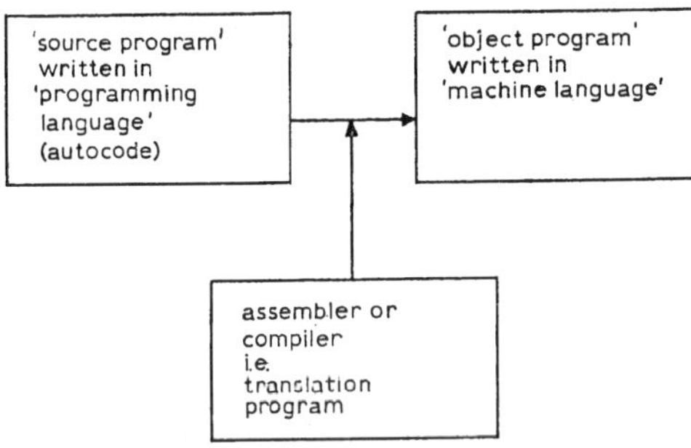

FIG. 6

The most widely used autocodes are undoubtedly those which go by the names of ALGOL, FORTRAN and COBOL, all of them originally developed in the late 1950s. ALGOL (short for ALGOrithmic Language) was designed for scientific mathematical calculations and became rapidly accepted on an international scale. FORTRAN (short for FORmula TRANslation) is also scientifically oriented, while COBOL (short for COmmon Business Oriented Language) was developed specifically for business purposes. They are all three translated by compilers.

Although the use of an autocode simplifies the job of programming, the problem of conceiving the pattern or form of a program as a whole remains.

Usually, before detailed writing of a program commences, the programmer finds it convenient to draw up a diagram showing the overall organisation of the computation. This helps to clarify the situation and can save a great deal of time in programming especially where the eventual program is highly complex and where it would be difficult not to get lost in detail and hopelessly muddled without a general systematic guide. This sort of diagram is called a *flow diagram*, and one example of such a diagram has just been given (p. 60). Flow diagrams are also useful in explaining a program without going into programming detail which may not be of immediate interest to anyone except the programmer (and may even be a total bore to him).

One convention for flow diagrams is that actions are contained in boxes, decisions in boxes with curved end-walls, and stop/start instructions in circles. This is the convention adopted in this book.

FIG. 7

In order to write any except the simplest program one must be able to break down the total process into smaller steps which must be clearly related to each other, and divided into decisions and actions, as well as having a clear starting point and finishing point or points. When this is done more detailed programming can begin. To exemplify this process and to conclude the chapter, a flow diagram for running a bath is given in Fig. 8. This type of demonstration diagram is not exactly new, and others have been circulated for processes as diverse (or similar) as driving a car or having sexual intercourse. But it does demonstrate effectively the ideas involved in flow charting.

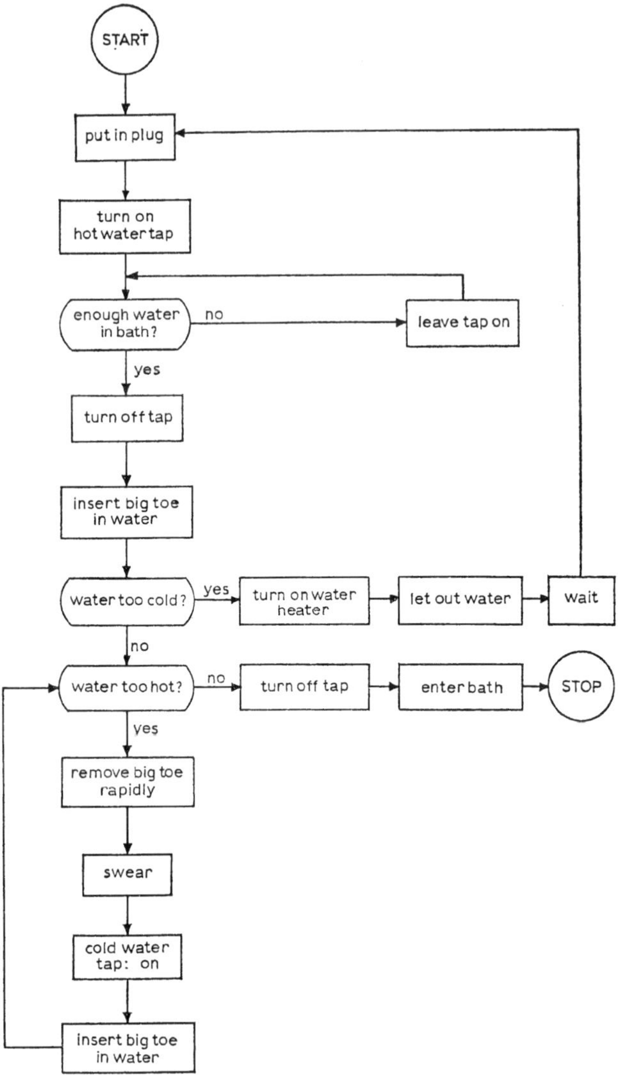
START
put in plug
turn on
hot water tap
enough water
in bath?
no
leave tap on
yes
turn off tap
insert big toe
in water
water too cold?
yes
turn on water
heater
let out water
wait
no
water too hot?
no
turn off tap
enter bath
STOP
yes
remove big toe
rapidly
swear
cold water
tap: on
insert big toe
in water

FIG. 8

SELECTED REFERENCES

Bernstein, Jeremy, *The Analytical Engine* (London, Secker & Warburg, 1963).
Cluley, John C., *Electronic Computers* (Edinburgh, Oliver and Boyd, 1967).
Green, Bert, F., Jr., *Digital Computers in Research: An Introduction for Behavioral and Social Scientists* (New York, McGraw-Hill, 1963).
Hollingdale, S. H., and Tootill, G. C., *Electronic Computers* (London, Penguin Books, 1965).
Irwin, W. L., *Digital Computer Principles* (Princeton, N.J., Van Nostrand, 1960).
London, Keith, *Introduction to Computers* (London, Faber and Faber, 1968).
Maley, Gerald, A., and Heilweil, Melvin F., *Introduction to Digital Computers* (New Jersey, Prentice-Hall, 1968).
Scientific American: Information (London, W. H. Freeman & Co., 1966).

4

LEARNING

TURING'S TEST

An important paper published in 1950 did a great deal to precipitate activity on computer simulation and has had a continuing influence since then. This was a paper written by Alan Turing, whose work in other contexts has already been mentioned. The paper, entitled 'Computing Machinery and Intelligence',[1] was concerned with a question which has now become an old chestnut: 'Can a machine think?' (According to Anderson[2] more than 1000 papers have been published on the question since 1950.)

Turing suggested that a useful way to deal with this question would be the following. There is a game played at parties called the 'imitation game'. (Turing must have been to some desperately tedious parties.) A man and a woman are hidden from view in some way, but are still able to communicate with an interrogator. The interrogator asks them questions (any kind) and their replies may or may not be truthful. The aim of the game is for the interrogator to guess which of the people he is interrogating is the man and which the woman. In order not to make the game too easy, communication is in writing or, better, typed.

Turing now suggests that the same game could be played with the interrogator having to distinguish not between a man and a woman but between a human being and a computer. If, over a number of trials with different interrogators, interrogators are

[1] Turing A. M., *Mind* (October 1950), **59**, 433–60.
[2] Anderson, Alan Ross, Introduction, in *Minds and Machines*, Ed. Anderson, A. R. (New Jersey, Prentice-Hall, 1964).

found to have succeeded in their guesses no more than one would expect on a chance basis, then it can be claimed that the computer thinks. Putting the test in this way gets rid of superficial or trivial differences between man and machine and allows one to make a decision purely on the evidence of the thinking itself.

As far as I know, no one has yet tried to carry out Turing's test, as it has come to be called, with a computer. But the test itself has received a good deal of attention in papers dealing theoretically with this issue.

Turing's contribution in this paper was not only to propose this test, but also to put forward an argument which has been debated widely since, to the effect that in due course it should be possible to program a computer to pass the test. The argument, briefly, goes something like this. Certainly there is a sense in which a computer will only do what we tell it to do (through the program and data). But a similar situation obtains with human beings. In fact three things determine the thought processes of a particular human brain:

(1) The initial state of the mind, say at birth.
(2) The education to which it has been subjected.
(3) Other experience, not to be described as education, to which it has been subjected.

In other words the human brain is also programmed—by genetics, education and experience.

Now there is no reason why a computer should not be programmed in the same kind of way. A basic program could be written for the computer, representing its child-brain, and specifying in particular how to learn. One could then go about educating it by giving it as input a vast amount of information which it would organise and utilise by means of the original program. The computer would also be allowed to learn for itself through interactions with its environment and given the possibility of asking questions.

Turing is arguing that there need be no difference in principle between the organisation of information processing in the computer and in the human brain. If one was to program a computer to learn for itself how to do something (i.e. program it with a 'child-brain' rather than an 'adult-brain') and if one was to input something like the same amount of information a human receives, both formally and informally, throughout childhood, then we should have a chance of producing a computer which would be able to pass the test he proposes for it. Of course, computers would have to have much larger memory stores and much better information input facilities than they have at present. But Turing regards such problems as essentially engineering problems, and problems which will sooner or later be overcome—his argument is at the more philosophical level of what is and is not in principle possible.

There are obvious objections that can be made to the argument. For one thing it begs the question: if the brain is a machine, then we should be able to get a computer to behave as the brain does. But the objection many people have to the idea of a computer thinking is the belief that the brain is not just a machine. (The opposite argument that defines thinking at the outset as a uniquely human ability also of course begs the question.) Again, one could imagine a computer programmed to pass the test in a way which clearly does not resemble the way in which the brain functions—for instance a huge dictionary of answers to questions might well work, at least for a time. In this case would one really be justified in saying that the machine was thinking? Should not any criterion for thinking include reference to means as well as ends?

Be this as it may, Turing's paper was important in that it stimulated many people to think more seriously about computer simulation, and especially about how far it would be possible to program a computer to learn, since learning seems to be the key to so much else. In the rest of this chapter we shall be looking at learning programs as such. But a number of the programs to be described in later chapters incorporate some kind of learning and in this sense are not completely pre-programmed but to some extent self-programming. The possibility of such machine learning obviously has important consequences for research in artificial intelligence as well as computer simulation.

SOME SIMPLE LEARNING PROGRAMS

It is simple enough to program a computer to produce behaviour equivalent to classical conditioning and operant conditioning. Thus, for classical Pavlovian conditioning of an on-line computer, all that is needed is for the computer to be programmed firstly to produce a given output number whenever a given input number is received (this representing an unconditioned reflex), secondly to record in the memory store all immediately preceding or following input numbers, and thirdly to produce the original output number in response to any input numbers which tend to occur as shown in the memory store before or after the original (unconditioned) input number. Parameters can be chosen which specify the number and pattern of pairings required for 'conditioning' to occur and, if a figure is added to output representing its strength, which specify this strength under different input sequence conditions. In this way, and with the addition of a number of further conventions, a faithful representation of the standard phenomena of classical conditioning could be obtained in computer form.

A program of this kind would also represent a simple kind of induction or concept formation in the sense that different inputs would in effect be classified together if they occurred in conjunction with a given (unconditional stimulus) input. In more general terms, the computer could be programmed to look for regularities in the form of patterns in the sequences of inputs and this leads into an important area of research: computer pattern-recognition. This will be considered further in Chapter 6.

Learning under the law of effect, i.e. instrumental or operant conditioning, can also be reproduced on a computer without too much difficulty. For example, in the simplest case all that is required is to arrange:

(1) that the computer prints out characters from a set of characters;

(2) in the memory store is a number related to each character which represents the probability of the computer choosing it at a given time and which governs this choice;

(3) this weighting number is determined by the proportion of times that the number when printed out has been immediately followed by a special input 'reinforcing' stimulus—the weighting could if required also be made a function of the delay of the 'reinforcing' stimulus and its 'strength'. 'Negative reinforcement' could also be programmed for;

(4) these weighting numbers are initially equal for all the characters so that the characters are initially chosen by the computer on a completely random basis.

Under these conditions, all one has to do is choose a character as an operant response and reinforce it every time it occurs in order to 'train' the computer to produce this operant. As long ago as 1952, in direct response to Turing's paper, Oettinger[1] programmed the Cambridge University EDSAC computer to learn to print whatever number the computer operator chose to reinforce, and to 'forget'

[1] Oettinger, A. C., 'Programming a digital computer to learn', in *Phil. Mag.* (December 1952), **43**, 1243–63.

if the reinforcement was not continued over a period of time.

The method used was somewhat more elaborate than that described above, but not fundamentally different. There was a set of response numbers together with the character *X* representing no response at all. Each response had to be elicited by an input 'stimulus' which was a number corresponding to the intensity of the stimulus. If the stimulus was not strong enough to elicit any response at all, then *X* was printed out. If it did elicit a response, then this response could be reinforced by the input of another number representing the strength of the reinforcement (or negatively reinforced by a minus number).

Each of the pool of response numbers had a weighting or 'threshold state number'. Initially all the weightings of the response numbers were the same. If a response number had a weighting which, when added to the stimulus intensity number at a given time, resulted in a sum which was greater than a fixed threshold number, then the response number was a candidate for being the output number at that time. The actual output number was selected randomly from the response numbers which satisfied the criterion just described. If none of the numbers satisfied this criterion, then *X* was printed out.

The 'threshold state number' of the response chosen to be printed out was then increased or decreased in accordance with the strength of the reinforcement or negative reinforcement which it obtained. Other factors were also programmed into the situation including random fluctuations in 'threshold state numbers' and a decay trend of all these 'threshold state numbers', the latter resulting in 'forgetting' if a given response which had been reinforced was not reinforced again from time to time.

A number of variations on this kind of program have been written, including attempts at accurate simulation of animal learning under the law of effect. A recent example of this is a program by Robinowitz[1] to simulate rats learning a simple *T*-maze for food reward in which one side is always rewarded and not the other.

Since the behaviour of rats in this situation is in fact variable, variability had to be included in the program: this was achieved by arbitrarily subjecting the momentary value of turning to either side to variation with a standard deviation of ·200. The computer had to make a random selection of a value for each tendency (left or right) on each trial from a distribution of values around the

[1] Described in more detail in Walker, Edward L., *Conditioning and Instrumental Learning* (California, Brooks-Cole Publishing Co., 1967).

mean value of each tendency. The computer then had to decide, on the basis of the higher value, which way the animal might be expected to turn. Under these conditions, over a period of trials one would expect the left turn and the right turn to be chosen roughly an equal number of times. However, the computer 'rat' was rewarded whenever it chose one of the sides. The effect of this was to increase the probability of the rat choosing the side rewarded according to a formula based on an exponential curve.

The result of this was to produce a learning curve similar to that obtained by real rats performing in *T*-mazes under conditions of low food deprivation and low reward. When four simulated rats were run in ten blocks of twenty successive trials the learning curve averaged for all four was, it was claimed, indistinguishable from results which might have been obtained with four real rats.

Computer models of learning of this type[1] of course merge into the growing field of mathematical models of learning.

In these examples of operant conditioning the animal is learning only a single response. Is it possible to teach a computer a *sequence* of responses? Again, there is no great difficulty in principle. Imagine, for example, that we wanted to teach a computer to play noughts-and-crosses successfully (i.e. so that it was never beaten). Plainly with such a simple game it would be possible to write a complete, algorithmic, pre-program that worked in this way. But we want the computer to learn such an algorithm for itself. This could be accomplished in the following way. We could label each of the 'squares' with a unique number for purposes of identifying the squares to the computer. The nought and the cross would also be represented by a number each and a 'board position' would describe which squares were associated with noughts and which with crosses represented in this way. We would then arrange for the complete board state to be read into the computer at each move and stored in the computer memory. The computer itself would be programmed to play its moves randomly at first but as the games succeeded one another, so the computer could examine its memory store to see if any board position which occurred had been previously encountered. If it had been and the game was subsequently lost, then a new move would be randomly selected for the current board position—otherwise the same move would be played again. It can be seen that, over a period

[1] See also, for example, Hoffman, Howard S., 'The analysis of discriminated avoidance', in *Operant Behavior*, Ed., Honig, Werner K. (New York, Appleton-Century-Crofts, 1966).

of games, poor moves would gradually be eliminated and eventually the computer would, if not winning every game, and no doubt missing opportunities, at least be unbeatable.[1]

It is obvious that the same sort of method could be used in the simpler situation of simulating a rat learning its way through a multiple *T*-maze. In fact, however, games like noughts-and-crosses, draughts and chess tend to be used fairly widely in computer simulation and in the field of artificial intelligence. This is partly because they represent *human* problem-solving situations which inevitably seem to us humans more interesting and less arbitrary than animal laboratory situations. They are also governed by clear-cut rules and objective definitions of success and failure, and this is particularly useful in comparing human and computer performance. Furthermore, human games are themselves in turn simple models of more complex real-life situations with less clear-cut rules and criteria of success.

LEARNING TO PLAY DRAUGHTS

When we get to the next level of difficulty, with a game like draughts (or 'checkers' as it is called in America), which is complex enough to preclude the practicable use of algorithms at all, then the computer *has* to be programmed to *learn* how to play the game if it is to play it at all successfully. And the learning has to be more sophisticated than the simple kind of learning involved in noughts-and-crosses. Let us look at one exciting approach to this: the draughts-playing program of A. L. Samuel.[2]

First, squares on the board and pieces are assigned numerical values which can be fed into the computer in much the same way as in the noughts-and-crosses program described earlier.

The basic strategy of the program is to use the technique of 'minimaxing', the idea of which comes from the Theory of Games[3] and was originally introduced into the field of computer game

[1] For a more detailed examination of the problem of programming a computer to learn to play this game see George, F. H., *The Brain as a Computer* (Oxford, Pergamon, 1961), ch. 6.

[2] Samuel, A. L., 'Some studies in machine learning using the game of checkers', in Feigenbaum, E. A., and Feldman, J. (Eds.), *Computers and Thought* (New York, McGraw-Hill, 1963). A not dissimilar approach has been worked out by Strachey. See Strachey, Christopher, 'System analysis and programming', in *Information*, Ed., *Scientific American* (London, W. H. Freeman & Co., 1966).

[3] von Neumann, John, and Morgernstern, Oskar, *Theory of Games and Economic Behavior* (New Jersey, Princeton University Press, 1944).

playing by Shannon.[1] The aim of the minimaxing strategy is at each stage to minimise one's maximum possible losses. That is, the strategy is based on the assumption that your opponent will always make the move that causes you the maximum loss (or the minimum gain) and so you have to choose moves which will make your position as good as it can be when your opponent has done his worst. The strategy is rather negative, especially if one is faced with an opponent who is far from perfect and does not always make his best move. But it is a good safe strategy to use.

How does one determine losses and gains in a game like draughts? Obviously piece-advantage is the main criterion: this is the number of pieces you have as against the number of pieces of your opponent. But there are other considerations like the degree of advancement of your pieces (because they become Kings when they reach your opponent's last row of the board), the amount of mobility in your position, and so on. Samuel chooses a number of these and provides ways of assigning numerical values or weightings to them. The result is that for each board position a single evaluation score can be computed. If this score goes down from one move to another, then one has made a loss: similarly if the score goes up one has made a gain.

Obviously in order to play the game at all intelligently it is necessary to look ahead and take into account the likely consequences of one's possible moves over a number of moves into the future. Minimaxing is therefore worked out over a number of moves ahead in Samuel's program. This look-ahead analysis gives rise to a tree-like structure, each of the nodes in the tree (representing a board position) being assigned an evaluation score. When evaluation scores have been computed for all possible board positions (or a subset of them) up to the number of moves ahead being examined, the safest course is worked out on the assumption, as we have seen, that your opponent will always make his best move (to your greatest disadvantage) at each stage. This necessitates working backwards through the tree from the most distant move calculated to the current move in order to select the current move. Let us look at what a simple tree of this kind might look like (Fig. 9). Two moves ahead are shown, the first one (row 2) showing scores after each of 3 possible moves are made, the second one (row 3) showing possible scores after the opponent has made his move. (The nodes in this

[1] See Shannon, C. E., 'Automatic chess player,' *Scientific American* (February 1950), **182**, 48.

case show *changes* in the evaluation scores, all the changes having the sign appropriate to the player about to make the first move.)

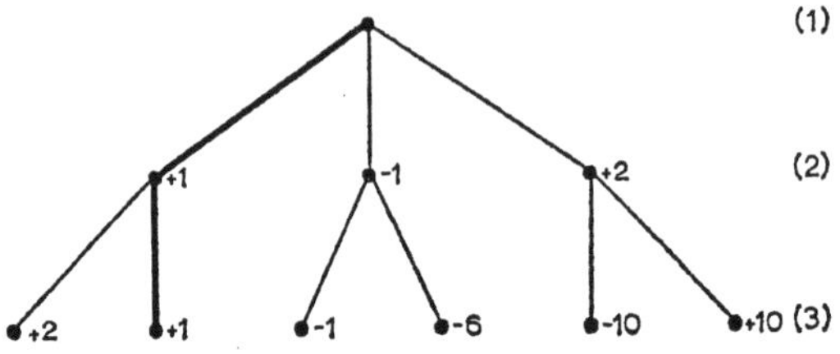

FIG. 9

It would seem at first sight, working back from row 3, as if the path leading to +10 should be chosen. However, if we are working on the basis that the opponent will always make his best move, from the +2 position in row 2 the opponent will in fact make the move that leads to −10. So making the immediate move that leads to +2, although this gives the best immediate gain and appears to lead to the best two-move gain, is in fact the worst move within the terms of this two-move analysis. The best move, and the path chosen by minimaxing, is marked in by a heavier line.

Using this strategy, the computer programmed with Samuel's draughts-playing program looks ahead a certain number of moves at a time. Ideally, it should be able to see right through to the end of the game, but this is rarely possible except near the end of the game because of the large number of possibilities (and then possibilities related to these possibilities etc.) which are generated. However, the computer could still work out more moves ahead in a given time than most human players, but this would reduce the interest of the program as a learning program (rather than as a largely pre-programmed method making use of the computer's computational speed). So playing time for the computer and the related look-ahead distance utilised by it are deliberately limited. Always a minimum of three moves ahead is worked out, but under certain specified conditions (e.g. if a jump can be made at the next move) a number of further moves may also be worked out.

Superimposed on this rather static basic strategy, Samuel provides two kinds of learning facility which lead to adaptation on the basis of experience and to improvement. These two methods have in the main been used separately by Samuel but they can be combined in various ways:

(1) *Rote learning*

The simplest form of rote learning is for each board position as it is come across in a game, together with its minimaxing evaluation leading to a particular move, to be stored in the computer memory store. Then when a position is met with in a subsequent game the memory can be searched for this position; if it is found a certain amount of computing time is saved which can be used to continue the minimaxing to a greater depth, i.e. over more moves ahead.

If board positions and evaluations are stored, however, an even greater advantage accrues (see Fig. 10). Suppose for simplicity that the computer always looks ahead by the fixed number of three

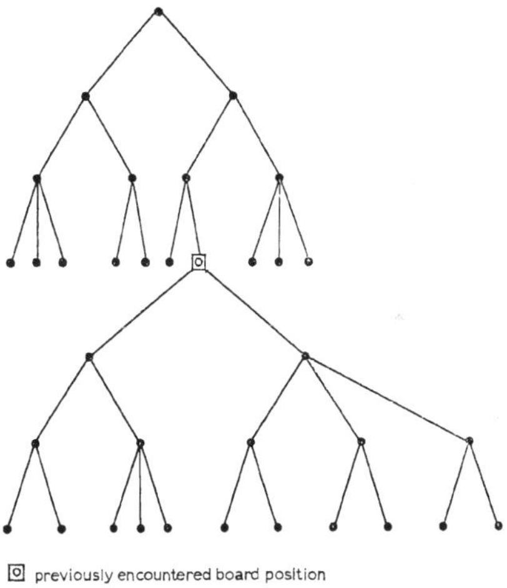

FIG. 10

moves. It can check its memory store to see if any of the possible positions in three moves' time are positions it has been in before in previous games. If they are, it can check the evaluations of this position, meaning that, in effect, it is looking ahead six moves (since the evaluations of this new position are themselves based on looking three moves ahead). If the computer does in fact choose a move which can lead to the position which has previously been evaluated, it can change the evaluation score of its current position to a six-move evaluation score and store it as such. This possibility of linking up evaluations in this way constitutes a powerful technique.

Board positions which are met with only infrequently are dropped out of the store. This 'forgetting' process by the computer enables available storage space to be used to the maximum advantage.

(2) *Learning by generalisation*

If the computer could make generalisations about the games it has played, even better use could be made of the storage space since all the detailed information about the board states would no longer have to be stored. More importantly, on the basis of such induction it should be able to determine which *general* rules or strategies are most likely to lead to success and hence to improve its performance continually.

Samuel has made a start towards this by arranging for the program to select the terms it uses in evaluating board states. Thirty-eight such terms are kept in storage and the computer selects from these sixteen to be used in evaluation at a given time. The decision as to which of these terms to use depends on the extent to which using them leads to success at playing the game. Each of the terms used is also given a weighting by the computer, using a special algorithm so that the extent to which each of them contributes to the overall evaluation of the board state can be made to depend on their apparent importance as determined by the previous success of moves in which they have been used. So the computer learns by trial and error which terms to use and how much weight each of them is to be given. Terms include: denial of occupancy, mobility, piece advancement and control of the centre of the board. One term, however, is always used, is used with a substantial weighting, and is not altered by the program: this is the piece-advantage term, i.e. the number of pieces owned as against the number of pieces owned by the opponent. In one sense this is the most important term since in effect it determines eventually who wins and who loses.

Minimaxing is then carried out by means of the currently used terms and their weightings, evaluation scores being made for the current board state, and then for subsequent board states which would arise from different moves being made, etc. If look-ahead of three moves is being used, the computer determines the most favourable (or rather, least unfavourable) board position in three moves' time and works back from this to the move that now has to be made. The evaluation score for the position in three moves' time is called the 'backed-up score' and is stored together with the evaluation of the current board position.

When the move has been made, the computer now compares (1) the backed-up score of the *new* board position with (2) the initial score of the *old* position before this move was made. That is, at each move the difference between the evaluation score of the board position before the move was made and the evaluation score of the board position in a few moves' time (worked out on a minimaxing basis) which is now possible having made the move, is worked out. This is used to determine whether the terms and weightings used in estimating these scores are satisfactory (as they would be if the game position is estimated to be improving) or unsatisfactory (if the position is estimated to be deteriorating). In the latter case the weightings are modified. The method of doing this, which is quite complicated, will not be gone into here.

As was mentioned above, not only are the weightings of the terms modified but also which terms are included in the active list used for evaluation is decided on the basis of experience. A term which is consistently found not to be satisfactory (in the sense described in the last paragraph) is replaced by the term at the head of the reserve list of terms and is itself placed at the end of the reserve list (and will in due course become a candidate for inclusion on the active list again).

In order to provide the computer with experience, Samuel used the ingenious idea of playing it against itself as well as playing it against human players. In due course the computer improved to such an extent that it was able to beat Samuel himself—a fact which has important implications for artificial intelligence if it is taken as a demonstration of the ability of a program to act more intelligently than the person who programmed it. The widespread idea that 'you only get out of a computer what you put into it' is then seen to be true in only a trivial sense.[1]

Samuel reports that the program was even able to beat a draughts champion. After the game (in 1962) the champion commented: 'The machine . . . played a perfect ending without one misstep. In the matter of the end game, I have not had such competition from

[1] Ironically, Samuel is one of the few actually working in the field of artificial intelligence to use the argument that computers only do what they are programmed to do, and that therefore they cannot be said to think: Samuel, A. L., Letter to the editor, *Science* (16 September 1960), **132**, no. 3429.

any human being since 1954, when I lost my last game.'[1]

This study is an excellent, indeed classic, piece of research on artificial intelligence.[2] Although its primary purpose was not that of simulation it is useful to ask at this stage about the extent to which the programs resemble the way in which human beings learn to play the game of draughts, or indeed the extent to which they resemble any kind of human learning in any situation. This is difficult to determine.

One immediate objection that occurs to one is to the terms used to describe the programs. But this does not in itself imply that the computer processes are not models of psychological processes that might go by some other name. Thus the term 'rote learning' in psychology is usually used, for example, to refer to the process by which human beings learn lists of nonsense syllables, and this bears little apparent resemblance to the process of rote learning in the draughts program. The latter involves in particular the linking of calculations to improve a decision which can be made at a given point. However, in this sense it may, at least in part, resemble the process of 'insight'—which has of course been described by Gestalt psychologists as the linking together of a number of elements in a situation to achieve a solution to a problem.[3]

Similarly, as far as learning-by-generalisation is concerned, it could be said that the program does not do any real generalising itself, but simply evaluates generalisations already formulated by the programmer. Human beings on the other hand do develop their own strategies rather than being given sets of strategies to choose between. However, it should be added that presumably human beings do also, consciously or unconsciously, develop 'feelings' about, and preferences for, different kinds of strategies and this, whatever term is used to refer to it, would seem to be the same process as that used in the program. The program may usefully draw attention to

[1] Samuel (1963), op. cit., p. 104.

[2] A more recent paper describes improvements which have been made to the program described here: Samuel, A. L., 'Some studies in machine learning using the game of checkers. II. Recent progress', *IBM Journal of Research and Development* (1967), **11**, 6, 601–17.

[3] De Groot, talking of chess, has argued that '. . . the difference in achievement between master and non-master rests primarily on the fact that the master, basing himself on an enormous experience, can start his operational thinking at a much more advanced stage and can consequently function much more specifically and efficiently in his problem-solving field'. De Groot, A. D., 'Thought and choice in chess', excerpt in Wason, P. C., and Johnson-Laird, P. N. (Eds.), *Thinking and Reasoning* (London, Penguin, 1968), p. 145. This would seem to refer to the effects of something like the same process as Samuel's 'rote learning'.

this aspect of human learning. Samuel himself points out, however, that the next step in the development of a human-like draughts-playing computer would be to enable it to learn terms and strategies for itself.

FURTHER RESEARCH

The few representative programs described in this chapter, and indeed all the programs written up to the present which incorporate learning, represent no more than a beginning in the simulation of learning—especially human learning. The question of generalisation and concept development in particular is a complex one which requires much further work, although a start has been made.[1]

There is also the question of memory and recall. One of the things which is so phenomenal about human recall is the way in which the brain is able to retrieve at least certain kinds of information from incredibly large amounts of information and do so almost instantaneously. If I say 'Give the name of a capital city beginning with the letter L' or 'Name part of a car' or 'Give an example of a piece of furniture' or 'What is the opposite of black?', responses come immediately. It is true that these questions are simple, but the amazing thing *is* just this: that to human beings such questions *are* simple. Information retrieval in computers programmed as they are at present will have to be improved considerably before they can begin to compete with human recall in this sense. A recent development which may in the future help in this direction is the advent of the possibility of making computers with a form of so-called 'content addressable memory'.[2] As we saw in Chapter 3, information is normally stored in computers inside locations with addresses and in retrieving information the computer does so by knowing the address; if it does not know the right address it cannot retrieve the information except by lengthy inspection. On the other hand, with content addressable memories of the kind now being envisaged, each location has a 'tag' which gives some information about the information contained in that location. That is, information is stored in locations labelled at least partly in terms of

[1] See Hunt, Earl B., and Hovland, Carl I., 'Programming a model of human concept formulation', in Feigenbaum and Feldman (Eds.), op. cit. See also Hovland, Carl I., 'Computer simulation in the behavioral sciences', in Berelson, Bernard (Ed.), *The Behavioral Sciences Today* (New York, Harper Torchbooks, 1964).

[2] Brown, Ronald, 'Novel artificial memories', *New Scientist* (6 March 1969), 502–3.

the information in them rather than in terms of arbitrary addresses. Obviously this can be a considerable aid in tracing information.

Presumably the fact that human memory appears to be based on rich associations among the material stored is also a factor in human information retrieval capabilities. The programming technique of list processing (to be described in Chapter 7, *Language*) provides the computer with the rudiments of a similar associative system.

Another difference between human and computer memory is this: computer memory as programmed conventionally is static, whereas human memory is dynamic. As psychoanalysts on the one hand and experimental psychologists like Bartlett on the other have shown, human memory is essentially active and is subject to distortions of different types: information it appears is assimilated to cognitive patterns and also transformed according to emotional evaluations. These may not be features that one would want to include in an artificial intelligence program—although if the brain is as adaptive and intelligent as it is commonly supposed to be they may well prove to have overriding advantages if one could but fathom them. But computer simulation programs involving memory and recall will have to be more active and pattern-oriented than they have tended to be. There is however already at least one computer model which involves some kind of rationalisation (see Chapter 8, *Personality*).

Of course another aspect of the non-static nature of human memory is that of forgetting. Forgetting was programmed into both the Oettinger and the Samuel programmes described in this chapter and has in fact been a fairly standard feature in many learning models. A new theory of forgetting has been suggested in a model by Feigenbaum which simulates the rote learning of nonsense syllables. In this model, response information is not destroyed but, under certain conditions, it may be temporarily or permanently lost and inaccessible in a growing net.[1]

Models of the relations between learning and maturation are needed too. Turing oversimplifies misleadingly when he talks of the child-brain as if the brain at birth is a perfect and complete machine ready to learn: in fact the brain itself develops during the early years and it is therefore very difficult to a developmental psychologist to know if a given behaviour change in a child is due to learning or to the advent of a new stage in the maturation of the nervous

[1] Feigenbaum, Edward A., 'The simulation of verbal learning behavior', in Feigenbaum and Feldman (Eds.), op. cit.

system. Does a child begin to reason abstractly at the age of seven, as Piaget reports, because enough information has been accumulated to make meaningful induction and abstraction possible, or is it because the nervous system has reached a certain critical stage of development? It would be interesting to try models representing these two possibilities and various combinations of them to see which most faithfully appeared to reproduce the facts of cognitive development. Indeed, it would be worth while to attempt to simulate all Piaget's stages of cognitive development in terms of a program consistent with his own theory.

SELECTED REFERENCES

Hilgard, Ernest R., and Bower, Gordon H., *Theories of Learning* (New York, Appleton-Century-Crofts, 1966).

Hunt, E. B., *Concept Learning: An Information Processing Problem* (New York, Wiley, 1962).

Norman, Donald A., *Memory and Attention: An Introduction to Human Information Processing* (New York, Wiley, 1969).

Smith, Karl U., and Smith, Margaret Foltz, *Cybernetics Principles of Learning and Educational Design* (New York, Holt, Rinehart and Winston, 1966).

Stewart, D. J. (Ed.), *Automaton Theory and Learning Systems* (London, Academic Press, 1967).

5

PROBLEM SOLVING

To some people the term 'problem-solving' is more or less synonymous with that of 'thinking'. To others, 'thinking' includes much else besides including the processes of recognising problems, using language, being creative and original, evaluating situations and even being irrational. The term may also imply consciousness. Indeed, the answer that one gives to the question 'can a machine think?' may depend on how inclusive one makes the term 'thinking'.

In this chapter we are concerned with the basic topic of problem-solving as such. The following chapters are in different ways to do with thinking in the broader sense: recognising and creating patterns using language, forming attitudes, and so on. The work we shall be looking at in these later chapters may be regarded as in part an attempt to show that however widely one defines the term 'thinking' computers can still satisfy the definition; that is to say, however tough one makes the questions in Turing's test the computer would still pass them. The question of consciousness of course cannot be dealt with in this way and Turing's test methodologically excludes the question in a typically behaviourist fashion; it is, however, a question of the greatest importance and it will be considered in the final chapter.

There has probably been more work in computer simulation on problem-solving than any other psychological process. Part of the reason for this may be that problem-solving is part of any definition of thinking, even the most narrow. But a more important reason is that in practice computer simulation tends to be related in one way or another to work in artificial intelligence and naturally more programs have been written in this field for problem-solving than for any other purpose. This topic has therefore assumed central importance in computer simulation too.

By problem-solving, of course, one intends to refer to more than the carrying out of mathematical calculations of the kind the computer was originally devised to accomplish. What one is referring to is processes like proving theorems, answering intelligence-test questions, playing games like chess, and so on.

HEURISTICS

An important distinction underlies the whole field of artificial intelligence and the computer simulation of thinking. This is the distinction between algorithmic and heuristic methods. (The former term was introduced in Chapter 2, *Cybernetics*). An algorithm is, as we have seen, a set of rules which, if followed literally, will achieve a desired solution. A heuristic, on the other hand, is a set of rules which, if followed, may achieve a solution but cannot guarantee doing so.[1]

Heuristics are important to work on artificial intelligence for two reasons. The first is that they may be used in situations in which there are no known algorithms, so that a solution may be found which could not be found in any other way. For example, there is no known algorithm for a computer to play draughts and always win; but, as we have seen, methods may be used which give the computer a chance, and an increasingly good chance, of winning. So Samuel's draughts-playing program is an example of a heuristic program.

The second reason for the importance of heuristics to artificial intelligence is that, if used, they may save a great deal of computing time over algorithms. An example of this comes from the paper by Newell, Simon and Shaw[2] from which the whole idea of the opposition of heuristic and algorithmic methods in computer technology to some extent stems.

Newell *et al.* point out that it would be possible to prove a theorem in a deductive system entirely algorithmically in the following way: write down all known true expressions in the system, then work out all valid inferences from these expressions, until eventually, as

[1] See Polya, G., *How to Solve It* (New Jersey, Princeton University Press, 1954).
[2] Newell, A., Shaw, J. C., and Simon, H., 'Empirical explorations with the logic theory machine: a case study in heuristics', reprinted in Feigenbaum and Feldman (Eds.), *Computers and Thought* (New York, McGraw-Hill, 1963).

must happen sooner or later, the desired expression occurs (or its negation, which would prove that the theorem required is not a theorem in the system). They call this technique the 'British Museum Algorithm' which reminds one of the old idea that if monkeys were given typewriters to play around with randomly for an infinite time, sooner or later they would type all the books in the British Museum. Although such a technique for proving a theorem must eventually be successful, it is likely to be highly tedious and time-wasting. Heuristic techniques, which provide intelligent ways of aiming one's search in fruitful directions, are therefore far more appropriate. Newell *et al.* in this paper give an example of a heuristic program for proving theorems, and we shall look at their work below.

From the point of view of computer simulation, heuristics are important because it is believed that human beings tend to use heuristic techniques widely in problem-solving—indeed it is this aspect of human thinking which many people may be referring to when they say that humans do not think 'mechanically' but use their intelligence and insight. They achieve solutions to problems for which no algorithm is known (and indeed fail to solve problems, for example in mental arithmetic, for which simple algorithms exist). So computer programs must be programmed also to think heuristically if they are to be satisfactory models of human thinking.

Of course in one sense any computer program (which works) is an algorithm: it provides a set of rules (instructions) to the computer which the computer follows literally. It would therefore seem that a computer is necessarily algorithmic. However, there is no contradiction in the idea of such algorithmic instructions constituting, on another level, a heuristic. That is to say, the *general strategy* used in the program may be algorithmic or heuristic but in either case the details of the program must be put in algorithmic form. Presumably the human brain works in the same way. The functioning of the brain at the neuronic level must in a sense be algorithmic, even while the brain is, at a higher level, using heuristic thinking techniques.

THE GENERAL PROBLEM SOLVER

In 1956, the team of Newell, Simon and Shaw wrote a computer program which they called the Logic Theorist.[1,2] This program was

[1] Newell, A., Shaw, J. C., and Simon, H., 'Elements of a theory of human problem-solving', *Psychol. Rev.* (1958), **65**, 151–66.

[2] Newell, A., Shaw, J. C., and Simon, H., 'Empirical explorations with the Logic Theory Machine: a case study in heuristics', in Feigenbaum and Feldman (Eds.), op. cit.

the first heuristic program to be put on a computer and was one of the first major ventures into the field of what is today called artificial intelligence. It was this program, too, that gave rise to 'list-processing' computer languages (see Chapter 7, *Language*). We shall not consider this important program here but instead look at a later program called the General Problem Solver (GPS), written by the same team, which incorporates and extends many of the ideas of the Logic Theorist. GPS represents in fact possibly the most important attempt to date to use the technique of computer simulation in psychology.

The General Problem Solver program of Newell, Simon and Shaw[1] constitutes an attempt to construct a heuristic problem solving program which is general enough to deal with a variety of problems of different kinds. It does this by using certain general strategies which they believe are also fundamental to the way in which humans solve at least some kinds of problems. And the use of these strategies means in effect that the program is constructing its own specific program to deal with specific problems. In Chapter 4 it was commented that the next step must be to arrange for the computer to generate its own strategies. The General Problem Solver in a sense does this. It is not, however, a learning program in that the strategies used to build up subprograms remain the same throughout.

The program is intended to be both a simulation of human problem solving and an attempt to increase the range of artificial intelligence. 'The program ... maximally confuses the two approaches —with mutual benefit.'[2] As far as simulation is concerned, Newell, Simon and Shaw regard the program as embodying a definite theory of human thinking, and they compare the way the program deals with a particular problem with the way in which humans deal with the same problem, making great use of introspective reports by the human subjects.

The program deals with three kinds of symbols representing:

(1) *Objects* in the task environment which can characterise
  (a) the current situation,
  (b) the desired situation and
  (c) possible intermediate situations.

[1] This has been described in a number of places. A particularly clear description is: Simon, Herbert A., and Newell, Allen, 'Simulation of human thinking', in Greenberger, Martin (Ed.), *Computers and the World of the Future* (Massachusetts Institute of Technology Press, 1962).

[2] Newell, Allen, and Simon, H. A., 'GPS a program that simulates human thought', in Feigenbaum and Feldman (Eds.), op. cit., p. 279.

(2) *Differences* between pairs of objects.

(3) *Operators* which can act on, and change, objects to which they are applied.

For example, suppose that the problem is to demonstrate that from a particular expression in symbolic logic we can deduce another particular expression, the expressions in question together with intermediate expressions in the deduction are 'objects', specific 'differences' between expressions may be detected (e.g. the connectives may be different, there may be more terms in one than the other, etc.), and expressions are changed by being acted on by 'operators' which are in this instance the rules of deduction of symbolic logic. These rules in effect state equivalent expressions which may therefore be substituted for each other.

To give a simple example, the problem might be to show that the expression $A.\sim(\sim B.\sim C)$ can be deduced from the expression $(A.B) \vee (A.C)$.

(. stands for 'and'; $\sim$ stands for 'not'; and v stands for 'or'.)

The rules of logic for transforming expressions contain among others the following:

$$A \vee B \leftrightarrow \sim(\sim A.\sim B)$$
$$A.(B \vee C) \leftrightarrow (A.B) \vee (A.C)$$

($\leftrightarrow$ means that transformation can take place in either direction.)

So, starting with $(A.B) \vee (A.C)$ the program can, after identifying the appropriate rule, operate to produce the intermediate expression $A.(B \vee C)$. The latter part of this expression (with the necessary modification of the letters) can be operated on using the other rule to achieve the required expression: $A.\sim(\sim B.\sim C)$.

A wide variety of problems can be analysed as involving objects or sets of objects which have to be transformed, perhaps through a number of steps, into other desired objects or sets of objects by means of certain rules or operations. The problem is usually solved by deciding which operations to apply in which order. Examples might include transforming a set of paints and a canvas into a painting, transforming a list of lessons into a time-table, transforming a musical theme into a variation on that theme and transforming a mathematical formula into a computer program.

How can a computer be programmed to decide on the correct sequence of operations to carry out in a given problem situation (i.e. to write its own subprogram in this situation)? To simplify this problem Newell, Simon and Shaw choose problem situations, like the logic example given, where there are a finite number of clearly defined operations which can be brought to bear on the problem. What the GPS program does, basically, is to achieve a goal (if it is possible to do so) by means of setting up subgoals whose attainment leads step-by-step to the attainment of the original goal. That is, it carries out a means-ends analysis of the problem situation which involves seeking means to attain ends and setting up new subsidiary ends, which also have certain means, in order to achieve the overall end. In the simple example given the computer would have to set up the intermediate goal $A.(B \vee C)$ and apply the means of the appropriate operator to achieve this end. (It is also claimed that, consciously or unconsciously, much human problem-solving is of this type.)

Three types of goals may be dealt with by GPS:

(1) Transform object *A* into object *B*.
(2) Reduce difference *D* between object *A* and object *B*.
(3) Apply operator *Q* to object *A*.

For example, the overall goal in the logic example given is that of transforming one expression (*A*) into another (*B*). This goal is a type one goal (in the list above). To do this, the computer matches the two expressions and detects a set of differences. It chooses one of these differences and then sets up a subgoal to reduce this difference. This subgoal is a type two goal. If it succeeds, a new expression (say *C*) has been set up which is less different from *B* than *A* was. Now a new type one goal is set up: to transform *C* into *B*. (This may of course require a whole sequence of further intermediate expressions before *B* is reached.) If, however, the subgoal had failed to reduce the difference between *A* and *B* (i.e. *C* is as different as *A* was), then another of the differences between *A* and *B* is selected and the type two subgoal is set up of reducing *this* difference. This time a new expression *D* is derived which is matched with *B* and a new set of differences detected which should be smaller in number or simpler to reduce if *D* represents a successful transformation.[1]

[1] Reducing one of a set of differences may well increase other differences. For example, applying the rule $A \vee B \leftrightarrow \sim(\sim A . \sim B)$, in order, to change signs ($\sim$) also involves interchanging the connectives $\vee$ and . and this may increase the differences between the two expressions. (This is rule 5 in the table below.) So it does not follow that because a difference is reduced the new expression is necessarily more similar to the desired expression than the initial expression.

Thus a type one goal gives rise to a type two goal which in turn gives rise to a new type one goal.

If enough type two goals are achieved, then the original, overall, type one goal should eventually be accomplished if this is logically possible. But how are the type two goals achieved: that is, how is a difference actually reduced? The answer is that a table is provided for GPS which for a particular kind of task, like deducing one expression from another in logic, relates operators and differences: that is, the table lists, for each difference, operators that are relevant to it. Such a table is in a sense external to GPS and simply represents, for the kind of task that GPS faces at a given time, what the environmental relationships are. This does not mean that GPS is not general, but simply that it has to have particular kinds of information to solve particular kinds of problems: if the problem is a logical one it needs to have a table relating the rules of logic to the kinds of changes which their application involves. This table as used in GPS is given below. Other tables might be provided for other situations, e.g. trigonometry.

	R1	R2	R3	R4	R5	R6	R7	R8	R9	R10	R11	R12
add terms			X				X		X	X	X	X
delete terms			X				X	X			X	X
change connective					X	X	X					
change sign					X							
change lower sign		X			X	X						
change grouping				X			X					
change position	X	X										

FIG. 11

In this table, the twelve rules of logic (operators) used are listed at the head of each column and the changes they involve (differences) at the beginning of each row. For example, rule 3 is:

$$A.A \leftrightarrow A$$
$$A \vee A \leftrightarrow A$$

and this relates to both adding and deleting terms. Similarly, there are two rules which give rise to a change of position:

Rule 1 $A.B \rightarrow B.A$

$A \vee B \rightarrow B \vee A$

Rule 2 $A \supset B \rightarrow \sim B \supset \sim A$

So once a difference is selected to be reduced, an operator which involves this difference can be selected to be applied, e.g. if the difference to be reduced is that the terms are on different sides of the main connective, then rule 1 or 2 might be applied. The subgoal is now set up of applying, say, rule 2 to the expression. This is a type three goal.

So far we have seen that the situation can be represented by a simple hierarchy of goals, the overall goal being a type one goal, this giving rise to type two subgoals and type two subgoals in turn giving rise to sub-subgoals of the type three variety. To transform an expression into another we have to reduce differences between the two expressions and to reduce differences we have to apply operators which do indeed reduce the differences. If the operator cannot be applied, then a new operator is chosen; this is analogous to the higher level, where if a difference cannot be reduced, a new difference is chosen.

However, when we ask how a type three goal is accomplished, the situation becomes more complicated, because the rule may not apply exactly to the expression. For example, suppose the attempt is being made to apply rule 7 to the expression $A \supset (B \supset \sim C)$. Rule 7 is:

$$A.(B \vee C) \leftrightarrow (A.B) \vee (A.C)$$
$$A \vee (B.C) \leftrightarrow (A \vee B).(A \vee C)$$

The attempt must now be made to transform $A \supset (B \supset \sim C)$ into, say, $A.(B \vee C)$. This is a type one goal which again in turn generates type two goals which in turn generates type three goals. So the different goal types again become applicable but at a lower level of the goal hierarchy. If the lowest type three goal is successful, then the expression becomes one which is transformed into an expression which the type three goal at the higher level can act on, which in turn reduces the difference and spells success at a yet higher level of the hierarchy. Methods are therefore used by the program in the course of using these very same methods. Self-referential situations of this type are called '*recursive*' in programming.

Thus the overall problem of transforming expression A into expression B can give rise to hierarchies of subgoals of all three of the goal types listed. Such a hierarchy can be envisaged as a tree-like structure, each difficulty encountered giving rise to a new branch. An executive program is used by GPS to decide on the development of this structure, e.g. whether to follow up a new branch when a difficulty is met with or whether to return to some earlier stage and follow through a new route. This involves answering such questions as: If an operator cannot be applied should the expression be transformed or should another operator be used? If an attempt to reduce a difference fails should another attempt on this difference be made or another difference chosen? If another operator is to be used, which one should it be? If another difference is to be tackled, which one should it be?

In order to make decisions about such questions, the GPS executive program is able to decide on the relative difficulty of differences by referring to the table of operator-difference connections. In this table the differences which are most difficult to reduce (like 'add terms') are listed first and easy differences (like 'change position') last. It uses this to judge at a given level whether the transformations are proceeding in a profitable direction: if the differences of new expressions generated are becoming more difficult to reduce, then clearly a new direction must be taken. Similarly, if in going down the hierarchy of goals, a subgoal is more difficult than a supergoal, the executive discontinues this subbranch of the tree and takes up the problem again at a higher level. Two other considerations also lead to a branch being discontinued (e.g. an operator being given up and another operator chosen): there is simply a limit to the length of a branch which the executive will allow, so that no branch can be more than this length, and if a new goal is identical to a goal already generated at a higher level this means that the search has turned into a recurring circle which it is fruitless to continue. Finally, in deciding which of a set of differences to attempt first, the GPS executive chooses the most difficult one first, expecting to find easier ones as it goes along.

In examining the introspective reports of subjects trying to solve the same problems as GPS the same processes can be seen repeatedly: the generation of intermediate goals, the attempt to convert expressions so that rules can be applied to them, the decision not to continue with a line of development if it becomes too far removed from the main line of thought, and so on. For stretches GPS and the human even make the same decisions. The authors of GPS claim in fact that '. . . no one has proposed any major alternative theories that provide anything like a comparably detailed explanation of human problem-solving data'.[1] This does not mean that differences between human and computer strategies do not exist. For example, human subjects seem to handle some sets of items in parallel, whereas GPS is entirely sequential.[2] But recognition of such differences leads to attempts at further improvement of GPS, and a number of additions to the basic GPS program have been made at different times for different purposes.

Although GPS may be a good model of human problem-solving in certain specific areas, it is far from clear just how good a model it is of human problem-solving in general. In fact the *General* Problem Solver may not in itself be quite as general as it was originally hoped it would be. Newell, Simon and Shaw themselves have concentrated mainly on using GPS in the restricted areas of logic, algebra and trigonometry. But when we come to deal with problems which involve the use of natural language rather than a precise artificial language, or problems of an artistic nature, or problems which have a large component of uncertainty, or problems which essentially involve the disentangling of relationships between the elements of a situation in order to understand it better (e.g. to build up rather than apply a difference-operator table), then further research needs to be done before we can tell how useful the GPS model is likely to be. Despite this it must be said that GPS already represents a landmark in the development of both artificial intelligence and the modelling of human problem-solving, a major step forward in both the synthesis and simulation of intelligent thinking.

Ray has said of the Logic Theorist, and the same applies to the General Problem Solver: '[It] makes at least two general contributions to the psychology of thinking: it shows that the complex processes of problem-solving can be compounded out of elementary processes, and shows that such elementary processes can solve difficult problems, thus taking away the "mystery" component of people's attitudes toward problem-solving.'[3]

A GEOMETRICAL THEOREM-PROVING PROGRAM

Another example of a theorem-proving program is that of Gelernter.

Gelernter points out that a heuristic is effectively a filter interposed between a solution generator and a solution evaluator for the type

[1] Newell, A., and Simon, H. A., 'GPS, a program that simulates human thought', op. cit., pp. 292–3.
[2] ibid., p. 292.
[3] Ray, Wilbert S., *The Experimental Psychology of Original Thinking* (New York, Macmillan, 1967), p. 91.

of problem being dealt with. Possible solutions are generated by part of the system and these possible solutions evaluated as to whether they are genuine solutions by another part of the system. If the solutions are generated on a random basis, the process is highly time-consuming. If a heuristic filter is inserted, then the possible solutions are thinned out before being evaluated. (Thus in GPS various criteria are applied to each new expression formed to see whether the new expression is more or less difficult than the previous expression—if more difficult then this line of attack is dropped.)

Gelernter makes deliberate use of this idea in his geometrical theorem-proving program.[1] The aim of this computer program is to discover proofs for theorems in elementary Euclidean plane geometry.

The problem, as with proving a theorem in symbolic logic, is to produce a sequence of statements (in this case using the symbols of geometry), the first statement being an axiom or previously established theorem of the system, the last one being the statement which it is desired to prove. The rules of deduction of Euclidean geometry are used to get from one statement to another. So the program must choose from its stock of axioms and theorems (which are given to it at the start) the appropriate ones for the particular proof being attempted, and then generate the remaining statements necessary to complete the proof.

Now a highly time-consuming 'British Museum' type of algorithm could be used to generate sequences of statements randomly on the basis of the rules of deduction, each sequence being examined to see if it leads to the required theorem. However, Gelernter programs the computer to work backwards from the theorem: in this way every sequence it considers does terminate in the required theorem. This in itself is not a great advantage over working forwards since each sequence generated, while at least terminating in the statement required, is not guaranteed to be a proof at all—and indeed most of such sequences will be false. The advantage is that working backwards allows a heuristic filter to be used. That is to say, the computer uses a heuristic for estimating the correctness of any statement generated, and if the statement appears to be false then the statement is rejected, and a new path backwards must be followed. This filter cuts down considerably the number of routes generated by the computer and hence directs the research in a generally more fruitful and less time-consuming direction.

[1] Gelernter, H., 'Realization of a geometry-theorem proving machine', in Feigenbaum and Feldman (Eds.), op. cit.

The heuristic filter makes use of a geometrical diagram of the problem situation. As Gelernter points out, virtually no one would attempt the proof of a theorem in geometry without first drawing a diagram. A deliberate effort is made to avoid coincidences in the figure which would weaken the heuristic, and therefore reasonably safe inferences can be made from it. (Actually, the computer does not literally draw such a diagram, but works out statements that could be drawn from it like 'Segment *AB* appears to be equal to segment *CD* in the diagram.') All statements generated by the theorem-proving part of the program are checked against the diagram, and any statements that appear to be false in these terms are rejected.

Using methods of this kind, Gelernter's program has been fairly successful. It has in fact managed to produce more than fifty proofs.[1]

OTHER EXAMPLES OF PROBLEM-SOLVING

Although theorem-proving has been one of the main areas of research in artificial intelligence and computer simulation, a number of other human problem-solving situations that seem to require heuristics have been investigated. From the large number of programs that have been written here, let us select and glance at several examples.

First let us look at a program designed to solve certain kinds of intelligence-test problems. One type of item which is found widely in intelligence tests is of the following form, which requires reasoning by analogy: *A* is to *B* as *C* is to (D_1, D_2, D_3, . . . D_n). For example: Black is to White as High is to . . . Higher, Green, Low, Top; 3 is to 9 as 4 is to . . . 3, 9, 10, 16, 40. Geometric figures are also sometimes used, as in the following diagram:

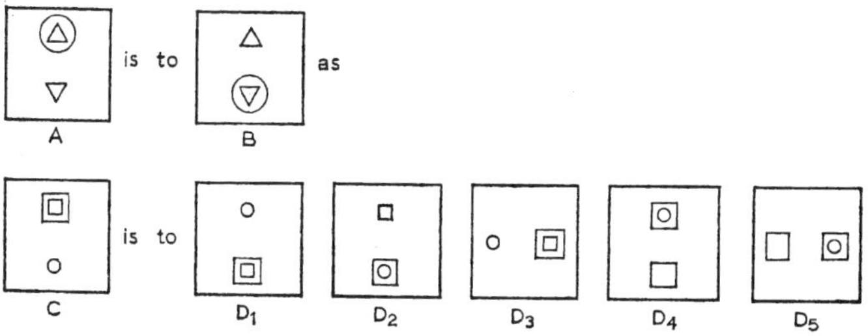

FIG. 12

[1] Gelernter, H., Hansen, J. R., and Loveland, D. W., 'Empirical explorations of the geometry-theorem proving machine', in Feigenbaum and Feldman (Eds.), op. cit.

A computer program has been written by Thomas Evans[1] to solve intelligence-test problems of just this type in geometric form. This program also constitutes a theory of the way in which the human brain deals with this type of problem, and suggests that four steps are involved:

(1) *A* and *B* are compared and the actions necessary to transform *A* into *B* listed, e.g. in the geometric problem shown, the circle around the top triangle is removed and this same shape is put around the bottom triangle.

(2) Similarities between *C* and *A* are listed, e.g. in the same problem, the top shape is enclosed in another shape.

(3) In each of the *D*s, features are listed that may relate the figure to *C* in the same way in which *B* is related to *A*, e.g. in D_1 in the same problem the small square has changed places with the circle and the enclosing square has moved from above to below.

(4) The *D* selected as the answer is the *D* which most closely matches in its relations to *C* the way in which *B* is related to *A*.

By breaking down the problem in this way it becomes evident that it is amenable to computerisation. The program which models this type of thinking is nevertheless a complex one. Briefly the information which the computer works with is in the form of descriptions of the shapes comprising in turn the figures *A*, *B*, *C*, D_1, D_2, etc., these descriptions being in terms of a graphical coordinate system (see Chapter 6). Relations between the shapes within each of the figures are worked out by the computer, these relations including 'inside', 'to the right', 'to the left', 'above' and 'below'. For example, in *A* in the example problem, one shape is inside the second shape and above a third shape.

In terms of these kinds of relationships the computer compares pairs of figures (*A* and *B*, *A* and *C* etc.), hypothesises the way in which *A* has been modified to reach *B* and selects a *D* with a similar set of transformations with respect to *C*.

Unfortunately, the program performance was not compared with human performance on these types of problems, but it would appear that the program can solve problems of a fair degree of complexity.

Decision-making under conditions of uncertainty is another

[1] Described in Minsky, Marvin, L., 'Artificial Intelligence', in *Information*, Ed., *Scientific American*, op. cit.

area of research in computer problem-solving. Feldman,[1] for example, has written a program to simulate the sort of problem-solving behaviour manifested in the 'binary choice' experiment. In this experiment the task is to predict which of two events (e.g. a + or a $\surd$) will occur on each of a series of trials, the subject being told on each trial after his prediction which event did occur. (In fact the series is random, but the subject is not told this.)

On the basis of observations of what subjects actually do in this experiment and also of the reasons they typically give for what they do, Feldman set out to produce a computer program which would simulate such human performance.

The resulting program consisted of a set of hypotheses about the pattern of events, e.g. that the pattern is a recurrence of $+\surd$ or a recurrence of $++\surd\surd$ or a recurrence of $\surd++$. A second type of hypothesis could be added to this hypothesis about the basic pattern of the events. This second hypothesis is what can be termed a 'guess opposite' hypothesis—this is based on the observation that human subjects seem to entertain a hypothesis that the experimenter will from time to time cause the pattern to be broken by giving the alternate symbol to that expected from the pattern so as to 'throw off' the subject. So the most general kind of hypothesis contains two components: a pattern component and a 'guess opposite' component.

The model itself operates in two phases, the first being concerned with explaining the preceding event, i.e. choosing a hypothesis which would be consistent with it, and the second with predicting the next event. If the computer decides that its current pattern hypothesis is to be changed, on the basis of the preceding event, then a subset of hypotheses (from the list of pattern hypotheses) which would be consistent with what occurred (making allowance for the 'guess opposite' hypothesis) is nominated, and one of these is chosen as the explanation of the preceding event. The one chosen in this way is the one that has been selected most often on preceding trials. The prediction of the next event takes this explanation hypothesis as its basis, and determines according to various tests whether to 'guess opposite' for this next event or not.

The detailed program was in fact built up from, and designed to simulate the behaviour in the problem situation of, a particular subject. Not surprisingly, perhaps, it appeared to be able to do this with reasonable accuracy. Feldman points out, however, that it is

[1] Feldman, Julian, 'Computer simulation of cognitive processes', in Borko, Harold (Ed.), *Computer Applications in the Behavioral Sciences* (New Jersey, Prentice-Hall, 1962).

difficult to measure the degree of consistency between the behaviour of the computer and the human subject. Thus the use of a simple 'difference count' which compares the corresponding decisions (hypotheses and predictions) of each system (computer and human) and counts the number of times they are different can make the two systems appear to be more dissimilar than they really are. This is because the model's decisions depend to a great extent on previous decisions it has made, and if one of these is different from the subject's then later decisions may differ too. So a difference between model and subject at a given time may be due not to any difference of overall strategy but to earlier decision differences. Something more general like Turing's test could be used, but Feldman argues that such a test lacks the rigour one would like to be able to apply and provides no precise way of *measuring* the degree of consistency between the two systems. Feldman in fact decides that the best solution is to use a conditional prediction procedure which involves using a difference count but setting the program back on the same track as the subject every time the two differ.

Another area which one can classify as part of the broader area of computer problem-solving is that of game playing—which, as was noted in Chapter 4, is a particularly popular topic. A number of board games like draughts and chess[1] have especially received attention, and a program to play draughts was described in some detail on pp. 72–9. This program reminds us that learning is itself a form of problem-solving heuristic.

There is one respect in which all the programs referred to in this chapter fall down as models of human behaviour: they all pursue their various goals with a single-mindedness which is most uncharacteristic of human beings. In problem-solving situations we are all subject to inattention, distractability and daydreaming. One reason for this is presumably that at any given time a number of goals are queuing up for our attention and if temporarily we seem unable to achieve one it is natural that we turn, again temporarily, to others. If we really wanted to, we could program computers too to choose between different goals, and to vacillate between them under certain conditions.

A more dynamic conceptualisation of the way in which distractibility might occur is embodied in a computer model of Reitman

[1] A particularly entertaining paper on computer chess is Good, I. J., 'A five-year plan for automatic chess', in Dale, Ella, and Michie, Donald (Eds.), *Machine Intelligence 2* (Edinburgh, Oliver and Boyd, 1968).

et al.[1] This is based on the idea that programmes like GPS are too centralised and sequential to be adequate models and that one should conceptualise the individual person as a coalition of subsystems with interdependent, but not necessarily identical, interests. Argus, the computer model which is a result of this viewpoint, is highly parallel in function and can display under certain conditions something analogous to distractibility.

ARE THERE ANY LIMITATIONS?

A variety of examples of computer problem-solving programmes have been described in this chapter, showing that the computer can perform many more of the functions of the human nervous system than many people might initially have thought possible. However, there are still various arguments to the effect that there are inexorable limits on what a computer can do in the way of problem-solving, and this implies that its possibilities as a simulator of human problem-solving may be limited too.

One argument is that a computer cannot possibly display originality in solving problems. This argument is difficult to assess since the term 'originality' is far from clear-cut, although one can operationally define it in certain ways to suit certain purposes, as the constructors of creativity tests have done.

However, probably the main reason for denying originality to computers is that 'computers only do what we program them to do.' In one sense this is undeniable, but as we saw in Chapter 4 when considering Samuel's program, it is possible in another sense to get more out of a computer than one puts into it. There seems therefore to be no reason in principle why a computer programmed according to general heuristic principles may not, at least from time to time, solve problems in ways which were not specifically foreseen by the programmer. Some of the proofs of Gelernter's geometry-theorem proving machine were no doubt original in this sense.

The possibility of originality in problem-solving may well be enhanced by allowing the computer to make use of random processes and also by programming it to think analogically—and we saw on pp. 93–4 (Evans's program) that it is already possible for a

[1] Reitman, W. R., Grover, R. B., and Shoup, R. G., 'Argus: an information-processing model of thinking', excerpt in Wason, P. C., and Johnson-Laird, P. N. (Eds.), *Thinking and Reasoning* (London, Penguin, 1968).

computer to function in this way at least at a simple level.[1] Indeed, it might be instructive to see if one could put in program form the various kind of thinking by analogy which Gordon[2] has suggested are found in much original thinking.[3]

Of course the terms 'originality' and 'creativity' are used in everyday language especially with reference to the production of works of art. How far computers may be able to be creative in this sense is examined in the next chapter.

Another supposed limitation on computer problem-solving is that it is claimed computers have to be 'rational'. Again, the term 'rational' may be used in different ways. If it means 'deductive', we have already seen that computers, through learning, may function inductively. If it means 'deterministic', then it can be pointed out that random (or quasi-random) processes may be incorporated in computer programs. If it means 'non-emotional', then, as we shall see in the chapter on personality, computers may be programmed to develop emotional attitudes and also apply Freudian defence mechanisms to their information processing. If it means 'non-fantasy', then it is ironic that one fashionable theory of dreaming likens it to the process of clearing and revising computer programs.[4]

A more serious argument is based on the proof by Gödel[5] of his well-known 'incompleteness' theorem. This theorem states that any consistent formal system that contains the usual axioms of arithmetic is incomplete. By this is meant that there are propositions, expressible by means of the symbols of such a system, which are true but which cannot be proved to be true within the system; these propositions can only be proved to be true if the system itself is inconsistent. Another way of putting the theorem is to say that no

[1] The argument in this sentence has been presented in more detail in Scriven, Michael, 'The compleat robot', in Hook, Sidney (Ed.), *Dimensions of Mind* (New York, Collier, 1961).

[2] Gordon, W. J. J., *Synectics: The Development of Creative Capacity* (New York, Harper, 1961).

[3] For a further discussion of creativity in the context of information-processing models see Newell, Allen, Shaw, J. C., and Simon, H. A., 'The processes of creative thinking', in Gruber, H. E., Terrell, G., and Wertheimer, M. (Eds)., *Contemporary Approaches to Creative Thinking* (London, Prentice-Hall International, 1963).

[4] Evans, Christopher, 'The stuff of dreams', *New Scientist* (18 May 1967). See also Greenberg, R., and Dewan, E. M., 'Aphasia and rapid eye-movement sleep', *Nature* (12 July 1969), **223**, 183–4.

[5] The reference to this paper is given in Chapter 2. An excellent account of the theorem is given in Nagel, Ernest, and Newman, J. R., *Gödel's Proof* (New York University Press, 1958).

system can within itself show itself to be a complete system. A number of other logicians and mathematicians have proved similar theorems, including Turing in the paper (referred to in Chapter 2) in which he introduced the notion of an infinite automaton, or Turing machine.

It has been argued by a number of writers that an implication of Gödel's proof is that brains, or 'minds', cannot be explained as machines. For example, Lucas has claimed: '. . . we cannot hope ever to produce a machine that will be able to do all that a mind can do: we can never, not even in principle, have a mechanical model of the mind.'[1] The argument in support of this statement is, roughly, that mind must be more than a machine because mind can see that certain statements are true which cannot be proved by a consistent machine system. 'Thanks to Gödel's theorem, the mind always has the last word.'[2]

But why should 'mind' always have the last word? A machine might be able to recognise certain statements as true which cannot be proved consistently by a human being. Why should a machine not have the last word by picking a hole in any formal system presented to it by a human being, rather than the other way round? As Turing has said, referring to this kind of problem: '. . . there might be men cleverer than any given machine, but then again there might be other machines cleverer again, and so on.'[3]

The truth of the matter is surely that both men and machines are subject to Gödel's theorem, to the extent to which they operate as formal systems.

In general terms, Gödel's theorem refers only to consistent, deductive systems, i.e. algorithms. But as we have seen in this chapter, a mechanical system like a computer is not confined in its functioning to algorithms. Just like the human nervous system, both systems are at base algorithmic, obeying certain consistent laws, but at a higher level both may function heuristically. Both human beings and computers may overcome the limitations of Gödel's theorem under certain conditions by tolerating occasional inconsistencies and errors which are almost inevitable using heuristic methods, and both are ultimately subject to the limitations of this theorem.

[1] Lucas, J. R., 'Minds, machines and Gödel', in Anderson, A. R. (Ed.), *Minds and Machines* (New Jersey, Prentice-Hall, 1964), p. 47.
[2] ibid., p. 48.
[3] Turing, Alan, *Computing Machinery and Intelligence,* in Feigenbaum and Feldman (Eds.), p. 22.

SELECTED REFERENCES

Amosov, N. M., *Modeling of Thinking and the Mind* (New York, Spartan Books, 1967).
Arbib, M. A., *Brains, Machines and Mathematics* (New York, McGraw-Hill, 1964).
Collins, N. L., and Michie, D. (Eds.), *Machine Intelligence 1* (Edinburgh, Oliver and Boyd, 1967).
Dale, E., and Michie, D. (Eds.), *Machine Intelligence 2* (Edinburgh, Oliver and Boyd, 1968).
Feigenbaum, Edward A., and Feldman, Julian (Eds.), *Computers and Thought* (New York, McGraw-Hill, 1963).
Fogel, L. J., Owens, A. J., and Walsh, M. J., *Artificial Intelligence Through Simulated Evolution* (New York, Wiley, 1966).
Michie, D. (Ed.), *Machine Intelligence 3* (Edinburgh, Oliver and Boyd, 1968).
Reitman, W., *Cognition and Thought: An Information Processing Approach* (New York, Wiley, 1965).
Wason, P. C., and Johnson-Laird, P. N. (Eds.), *Thinking and Reasoning* (London, Penguin Books, 1968).

6

PATTERN: RECOGNITION AND CREATION

PATTERN-RECOGNITION

In comparing human beings with computers, it is startling to realise that certain data processing functions, like pattern-recognition and the use of language, which turn out to be highly difficult to program with success on a computer, are achieved with consummate ease by a young child. And yet other functions which are comparatively simple to program, like various mathematical calculations, are well beyond the reach of the mental arithmetic of even intelligent adults. In part this brings to our attention in a novel way the strange mixture of biological sophistication and primitiveness which constitutes the human being. A child by the age of two, for example, can already recognise most of the objects in his environment and is in the process of carrying out one of the most astonishing feats of biology: the learning of language. But this same child will be totally unable to understand various simple abstract concepts—he will not understand, for example, the unvarying nature of a given number (Piaget).

It also brings to our attention, conversely, the primitiveness of computers in one major respect: their insensitiveness to pattern. Human beings appear to be highly pattern-sensitive systems: they remember faces even though they forget the names that go with them. They read numbers with ease, even though they make errors in carrying out the ensuing calculations. Indeed, a human being spends his waking life immersed in vast quantities of information from all his sensory systems. He has to reduce this information to some manageable form and this involves the search for consistencies or patterns in the information which reduce its complexity. On this ability to discover useful patterns in short periods of time depends his continuance as a viable system. Computers, when programmed conventionally, are so insensitive to pattern that a slight error in the input can cause a total failure to the calculation. And the problem of selecting from incoming information rarely arises, the information usually being pre-selected and then entered sequentially through one limited channel. It is clear that if computers are to become more intelligent and adaptive and autonomous from an artificial intelligence point of view, and if they are to become useful simulators of all aspects of human behaviour, then they must be programmed and used for pattern-recognition. This endeavour is the subject of the first part of this chapter, the last part being devoted to pattern-creation. (That form of pattern-recognition and creation which constitutes language behaviour is so important in its own right that a chapter has been set aside especially for it.)

Pattern-recognition involves two things: an association such that a certain kind of perceptual stimulus, which might be complex, is related consistently to a certain response, or representation in the nervous system, e.g. one recognises that the two following letters are the same: *A,A*. Secondly, and this is what makes pattern-recognition so difficult to program, stimuli which are dissimilar in certain respects are still classified together: they produce the same response, or are represented in the same way in the nervous system. For example, ten letter *A*s hand-printed by ten different people are still recognised as the letter *A* and not as *B* or *C* or some other letter or configuration of stimuli. The latter is an example of a reduction of environmental complexity. Many others could be cited, like recognition of the same object from different angles and distances, recognition of the same tune in different keys, recognition of examplars of classes of objects like 'tables' and 'chairs', and so on. However, the problem of the recognition of handwritten letters is the one which has received most attention in computer studies, and has been treated as something of an archetypal problem in pattern-recognition.

The field of pattern-recognition by computer is a large one. A great proportion of this field, especially in the early stages of its development, had a practical orientation: it was concerned with programming computers to recognise printed letters, and also various auditory patterns, where these were presented in reasonably standard forms. This is obviously of great importance to computer technology, and the primary concern was naturally enough not that of programming computers to recognise patterns in the way that humans do.[1]

Among programs designed to simulate human pattern-recognition, several broad approaches have been followed. One approach derives from that part of automata theory which deals with networks. Now a network can be constructed in such a way that sets of inputs are in effect classified together in that they give rise to the same output. Furthermore, networks can be designed that can learn to classify together certain input stimuli (e.g. those that occur together at the same time). This can be done for example by arranging for the passage of stimuli in the network to change the thresholds of elements in the network. Learning can then occur even in networks which are initially randomly connected. Various programs representing such networks have been put in computer form, and interpreted as simulating networks of neurons in the nervous system. Among others who have written such programs have been Farley and Clark,[2] and Rosenblatt[3] who has worked with a class of random nets which he has called 'perceptrons'.

A second, and more recent, approach is one which can be characterised as 'feature detection'. Programs based on this approach, like those of Selfridge and Neisser and of Uhr and Vossler, have achieved great success at recognising patterns.

SELFRIDGE AND NEISSER

The aim of Selfridge and Neisser's program[4] is to enable the computer to recognise hand-printed capital letters of the alphabet. There is a wide variety of differences in the way in which people write letters. The very same letter may be written by different people in quite different ways: large or small, upright or slanted, tall or short, thick or thin. Indeed, each individual writes in a way which is unique to him. And yet, by and large, we are able to read each other's writing and recognise each other's hand-written characters. How can a computer be programmed to succeed in this formidable task?

[1] For an example of such a synthesis program see Weaver, J. A., 'Machines that read', *Science Journal* (October 1968), **4**, 10.

[2] Farley, B. G., and Clark, W. A., 'Simulation of self-organising systems by digital computer', *Trans. IRE Professional Group on Information Theory* (September 1954), 76–84.

[3] Rosenblatt, F., 'The Perceptron: a probabilistic model for information storage and organisation in man', *Psychol. Rev.* (November 1958), **65**, no. 6, 386–408.

[4] Selfridge, Oliver G., and Neisser, Ulric, 'Pattern recognition by machine', *Scientific American* (August 1960), **203**, 2, 60–8.

First of all, the perceptual data must be converted into a form which is acceptable as computer input. Selfridge and Neisser achieve this by splitting each character (on its background) to be recognised into a matrix of squares, each of which is either black or white—like a half-tone photograph—and this information can therefore be entered into the computer in binary form.

An obvious strategy to use next would be to attempt to match the whole of each character input with a series of templates. In practice this kind of strategy has been found to be inadequate, largely because different versions of the same letter may be less similar than completely different letters, as shown by the following diagram involving templates for the two letters E and R.

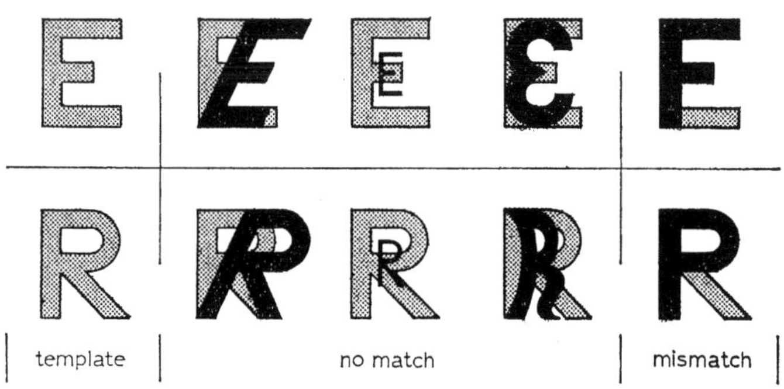

FIG. 13

Selfridge and Neisser use a different, although not entirely unrelated, strategy. This derives from the observation that letters can be described in terms of various *features*. (Indeed, if one was to try to describe a letter to a foreigner who used a different letter system it is probably such features that one would refer to.) For example, the letter *H* consists of two lines which are more vertical than they are horizontal, and one line which is more horizontal than vertical; it is also roughly concave at the top and at the bottom. All these features taken together specify the letter *H* more closely than any other letter. But one of these features alone is not enough: for example, *A* also has two lines which are more vertical than they are horizontal. If the computer is provided with information about the set of features which characterises each letter, it can use this for letter-recognition, matching the set of features of each sample letter to the features specified for each letter.

Two matching strategies now become possible. One is to use sequential processing in which the features are inspected one after another in a predetermined sequence, the outcome of each test determining the next step; e.g. if there is a concavity at the bottom then this delimits the range of possible letters that the sample could be and determines which next question to ask to limit the range of possibilities still further.

The second strategy, and the one used by Selfridge and Neisser, is that of parallel processing. This means that, in effect, all the questions are asked at once, the answers being presented together to the part of the program which makes the decisions about each of the sample letters. That is, a sample letter is described by the computer in terms of a combined set of features which it possesses. A flow chart showing how this method may be used to recognise the four letters *A*, *H*, *V* and *Y* is shown on p. 106. The apparently chaotic nature of this procedure has led Selfridge and Neisser to name their program, wryly, 'Pandemonium'.

The parallel approach has a number of advantages over the sequential approach. Perhaps one of the main ones is that in probabilistic situations, like the one being considered, sequential programs may need complex back-tracking facilities to compensate for erroneous decisions made earlier in a sequence. In any case, some features are not amenable to simple yes-no decisions. For example, it is difficult to decide whether the letter *B* has a crossbar or not: it is more nearly accurate to say that it has a certain degree of 'cross-barness'. So features, in Pandemonium, are assigned quantitative values and these are made use of in decision-making in a way which would be considerably more difficult with a sequential process.

This brings us to an important feature of Pandemonium: it can learn from experience. It does not assume that the features of a letter are unvarying in their presence, but that they have different probabilities of occurrence. So, when confronted with a particular sample figure, it makes a probabilistic estimate of which letter it is. And from experience it makes increasingly accurate probabilistic assessments. More specifically, what happens is that during a learning phase every letter presented to the machine is tested for *all* the features which can possibly discriminate between all the letters being 'taught'. (The computer has a dictionary of all these features.) Samples of each of the letters being taught are fed into the computer

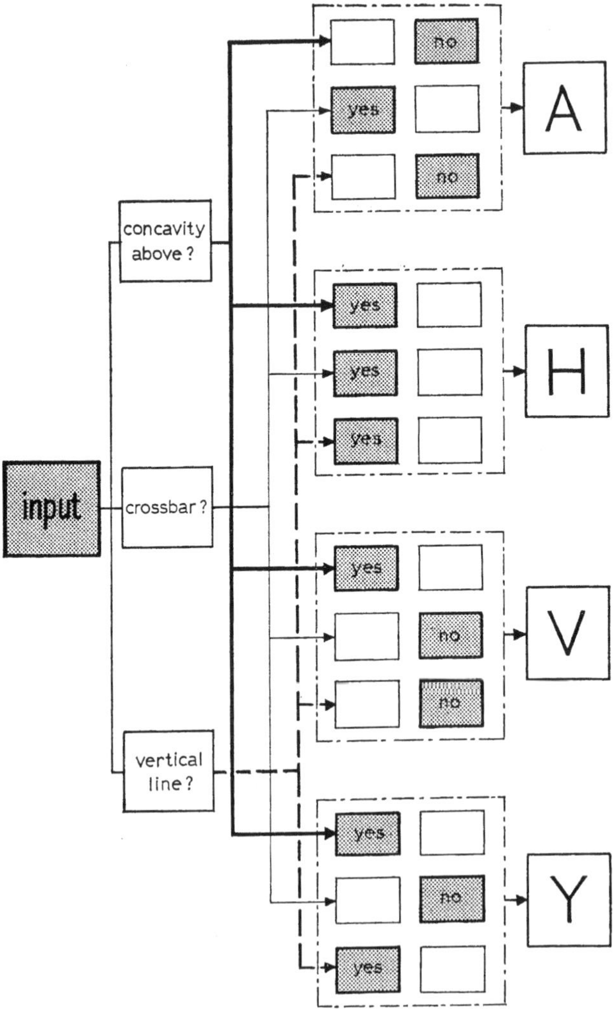

input
concavity above?
crossbar?
vertical line?
no
yes
no
yes
yes
yes
yes
no
no
yes
no
yes
A
H
V
Y

FIG. 14

and identified for it. On this basis the computer builds up a table showing how many times each feature was associated with each letter and therefore, for a particular feature, its probability of being associated with each of the different letters. The system is now in a position to attempt to recognise a sample letter which is not identified for it. What it does is to work out the list of features for the sample, look up the probabilities for each of these features being associated with each of the letters it has been taught in turn, and to compute (by adding probabilities) the probability of the sample being each of the letters in turn. The letter which it in fact finally recognises the sample as being is the letter with the highest probability value.

A version of Pandemonium to recognise ten hand-printed letters (*A, E, I, L, M, N, O, R, S* and *T*) and to improve with experience has in fact been run, and has been able to operate with an error rate of only 10% more than human subjects—a substantial achievement.

One thing which Pandemonium cannot do is to generate test features of its own. At the present time this kind of problem would appear to be the major one facing a great deal of research in artificial intelligence. Thus we have already seen this problem in the context of Samuel's draughts-playing program and Newell, Simon and Shaw's GPS (where the operator-difference table has to be provided for the program). Until it is solved, to quote Selfridge and Neisser, ' "artificial intelligence" will remain tainted with artifice'.[1]

Fortunately a sophisticated program by Uhr and Vossler has been written with just this aim of allowing the computer to generate its own test features for pattern-recognition. This program may therefore be regarded as an attempt to simulate perceptual learning.

UHR AND VOSSLER

Let us see first how Uhr and Vossler's program[2] functions in pattern-recognition in a pre-programmed way before we see how it can be made to learn to improve its performance.

First of all, the pattern to be identified is split into a matrix, just as it was with Selfridge and Neisser's program. The matrix

[1] Selfridge, O. G., and Neisser, U., op. cit., p. 68.

[2] Uhr, Leonard, and Vossler, Charles, 'A pattern-recognition program that generates, evaluates, and adjusts its own operators', in Feigenbaum and Feldman (Eds.), op. cit. A simpler description is given in Uhr, L., 'The development of perception and language: simulated models', in Tomkins, S. S., and Messick, S. (Eds.), *Computer Simulation of Personality* (New York, Wiley, 1963).

consists of 20 by 20 cells; cells covered by the pattern contain '1's and the rest contain '0's, as shown in the diagram.

A rectangular mask is then drawn around the input in such a way as to contain the whole input pattern in the smallest possible rectangular area.

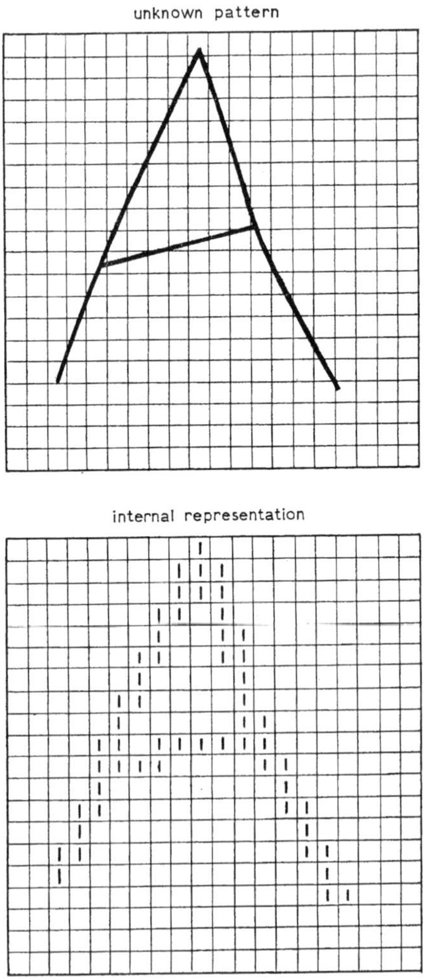

FIG. 15

A set of 'operators' are now applied to the resulting rectangular matrix. An operator is in effect a template to detect an element of a pattern. For example, one of these templates may be for a slight downward curve from left to right, another for an intersection between a horizontal and vertical line, etc. Each operator is much smaller than the total pattern, being a matrix of 5 by 5 cells. It is therefore set to detect features within the pattern, i.e. local characteristics of the pattern. A cell in the operator matrix can be in one of three states: '0', '1', or blank. Each of these template matrices is translated across and down the pattern within the larger rectangular matrix, cell by cell. Wherever it matches part of the input pattern the position is recorded. By 'matching' is meant that its '1's cover '1's and its '0's cover '0's (blanks are ignored). See Fig. 16. The operator at the lower left of this diagram is shown in the two positions where it matches the input matrix.

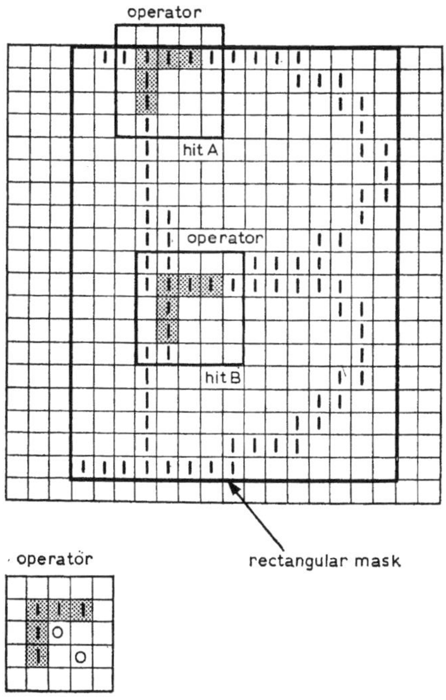

FIG. 16

This process is repeated for each operator in turn, each operator giving rise to a description of four 'characteristics' of the unknown pattern:

(1) The total number of matches that were found.
(2) The average horizontal position of the matches within the rectangular mask.
(3) The average vertical position of the matches.
(4) The average value of the square of the radial distance from the centre of the rectangular mask (which describes how central the matches were in the pattern). If a mask had not been used this characteristic would depend considerably on the size of the unknown pattern—a feature which is normally not of relevance in pattern-recognition.

There is also a second, higher-order, type of operator which may be used. This is a combinatorial operator which specifies two previously calculated characteristics which are to be combined by means of a specified logical or arithmetical operation taken from a list of sixteen such operations.

In this way, then, the operators transform the input into a list of characteristics (and also characteristics based on characteristics). This list is now compared with lists of characteristics in the memory store representing different patterns. The name of the list of characteristics most similar to the input list is then chosen as the name for the input list, e.g. if the name of this memory list is pattern '*A*' then the input pattern is identified as '*A*'.

Learning can now be programmed to take place on the basis of this pattern-recognition strategy. One way is this. The list of characteristics which has been generated by the operators for a given input pattern is examined by the computer. Amplifiers for each of the characteristics are then turned up or down depending on whether they contributed to success in identifying the input or not. This process of adjustment of the amplifiers leads in due course to discarding operators which lead to characteristics which are not useful in identification, and to their replacement by new operators. This in turn tends eventually to produce an optimum set of operators for processing a set of patterns.

This generation of new operators is a second way in which the computer learns, and it is here especially that the program represents an advance over, for example, Selfridge's 'Pandemonium' program in that it is developing its own test features. Each operator is in effect a string of twenty-five numbers which define the cells of the 5 by 5 matrix. There are various ways in which new strings can be generated. They can be generated randomly, although certain limits can be specified like the number of '1's which the string should contain. Or they can be 'extracted' from the input pattern under consideration. In this case templates are derived, according to a set of rules, from certain aspects of the pattern itself. This technique is particularly useful since it focusses the program on features which actually occurred rather than making it search through a much larger set of features which might occur, i.e. it functions as a heuristic filter.

The higher-order operators which combine characteristics are generated randomly by the program: that is, the two characteristics to be combined and the logical or arithmetical operation to be used are in each case chosen randomly. Each such operator is, however, tested before it is adopted, on two previous patterns stored in memory. The object of this is to choose higher-order operators which produce characteristics which tend to be invariant over examples of the same pattern but which vary between different patterns.

It can be seen that memory resides in three different places in the program: (1) in the lists of characteristics, (2) in the settings of the various amplifiers, and (3) in the set of operators currently in use. If memory in the first case is the result of a functional equivalent of 'learning by rote', the second two cases are more sophisticated in that they are the result of a kind of 'learning to learn' process in which the program examines its own pattern-recognition ability and attempts to improve it. It is this feature of the program which makes it especially interesting.

The program has been tested in a number of ways and with a variety of patterns including drawings of cartoon faces and objects, and spectrograms of speech, as well as handwriting. It has performed with great success in all these cases. For example, on its sixth pass through a twenty-six-letter alphabet of hand-printed capital letters (written by different people) it was 100% successful on known patterns and 96% successful on unknown patterns.

Its performance has also been compared with that of human subjects.[1] In this case 'meaningless' patterns were used so that both the computer and the human subjects were starting 'from

[1] Uhr, L., Vossler, C., and Uleman, J., 'Pattern recognition over distortion by human subjects and by a computer simulation model for visual pattern recognition', *J. Exptl. Psychol.* (1962), **63**, 227–34.

scratch'. Under these conditions the program performed considerably better than the humans: as a simulator of human pattern-recognition the program was, surprisingly, too good rather than not good enough.

Uhr and Vossler regard the program as a model to the extent of giving a neurophysiological interpretation to it. They argue that the 20 by 20 matrix can be regarded as a 'retina' (fixating an image) and a 5 by 5 matrix operator as equivalent to a 5 by 5 net of 'retinal cones' converging on a single output unit. The '1's in the net represent excitatory connections, the '0's represents inhibitory connections, and the threshold for firing the output unit is set at the sum of the '1's. The translation of the operator over the larger matrix simulates in sequential form the parallel placement of a number of nets of cones throughout the retina. On this model, each different operator is represented in the eye by additional connection patterns between input cones, each connection pattern converging onto its own output unit. They argue that this is consistent with what is known of the anatomy of the retina, with a matrix of cones in parallel which connect up to several layers of neurons.

The reader may wish to find out more about this large field of pattern-recognition by computer, and more exhaustive surveys have been given by a number of writers like White,[1] Uhr[2] and Hunt.[3]

PATTERN-CREATION

It has been pointed out many times that man is not only a pattern-seeking animal, but also a pattern-creating animal. Not only does he discover patterns already in the environment, he also imposes them on the environment. He is an artist as well as a scientist.

If one is to be permitted a vitalistic metaphor, it is almost as if the forces of pattern-creation which went into the biological development of each human being from a fertilised egg to a complex adult, overflow into all parts of the environment surrounding each human being. In non-vitalistic terms, the principles of organisation which control such biological self-complexing and pattern-generation may also apply to some extent to psychological development and to the

[1] White, Benjamin W., 'Studies of perception', in Borko, H. (Ed.), *Computer Applications in the Behavioral Sciences* (New York, Prentice-Hall, 1962).

[2] Uhr, Leonard, 'Pattern Recognition', in Uhr, L. (Ed.), *Pattern Recognition* (New York, Wiley, 1966).

[3] Hunt, Earl, 'Computer simulation: artificial intelligence studies and their relevance to psychology', *Annual Review of Psychology* (California, Annual Reviews Inc., 1968), **19**.

patterning of the environment by the individual. (It is a pity that we have no way of measuring 'pattern' analogous to the ways in which we can measure 'information'.)

Computer programs to generate patterns have been written for a number of purposes. For example, there are Julesz's well-known computer-generated patterns used in psychology experiments to study binocular depth perception.[1] There is also the large field of *computer graphics* which involves the development of techniques of man-computer interaction, usually via a cathode ray tube on which patterns are displayed by the computer and through which the human operator can enter new graphic information by means of a 'light pen'. A number of highly sophisticated techniques have now been realised in this field. For example, the General Motors Corporation uses a system for car body design in which the cathode ray tube displays a diagram of the car, and this diagram can be shifted, enlarged or reduced, rotated, or seen in a different perspective. The car designer can also alter features of the design, with the light pen, directly on the diagram.[2]

None of this is directly relevant to the way in which humans create patterns. However, there is a developing field of computer usage which does hold out at least the possibility of throwing some light in due course on human pattern-generation: this is the use of computers to produce works of art (using the term 'art' in its widest sense to include music and poetry as well as visual fine art). Although the primary aim of workers in this field is that of synthesis, i.e. to produce art, it is interesting to see to what extent such programs can be interpreted as computer simulations of human artistic behaviour. This in turn raises more general questions about the function of art itself.

Of all the arts, music is most immediately amenable to computer treatment because of its obviously abstract and mathematical nature. A great deal of computer music has now been composed. The best known work is that of Hiller and Isaacson (at the University of Illinois) which started in the mid 1950s.[3,4] Using the University's ILLIAC computer they achieved a varied body of musical material

[1] Julesz, B., 'Binocular depth perception of computer-generated patterns, *Bell System Tech. Jour.* (September 1960), **39**, 5, 1125–62. The techniques of computer generation of visual and auditory patterns have been well reviewed by White, Benjamin W., 'Studies of Perception', in Borko (Ed.), op. cit.,
[2] Developments of this kind have been reviewed by Sutherland, Ivan E., 'Computer inputs and outputs', in *Information*, Ed. *Scientific American*, op. cit.
[3] Hiller, L. A., 'Computer music', *Sci. Amer.* (1956), **201**, 6.
[4] Hiller, L. A., and Baker, R., 'Computer Music', in Borko, H. (Ed.), op. cit.

from which they selected, by unbiassed sampling methods, enough to form a twenty-minute composition which they entitled, suitably enough, the 'Illiac Suite for String Quartet'.

They used the general technique of programming the computer first to generate material on a random basis and secondly to test the material in accordance with various rules in order to reject material not conforming to the rules.

The computer was programmed to generate numbers on a random basis, these numbers being equated not only with musical notes but also with rhythms and dynamics. Each number was checked in turn by a series of tests representing 'rules of composition'; numbers found at the stage in question not to satisfy any of these rules were rejected. This kind of process can be represented in flow diagram form as follows:

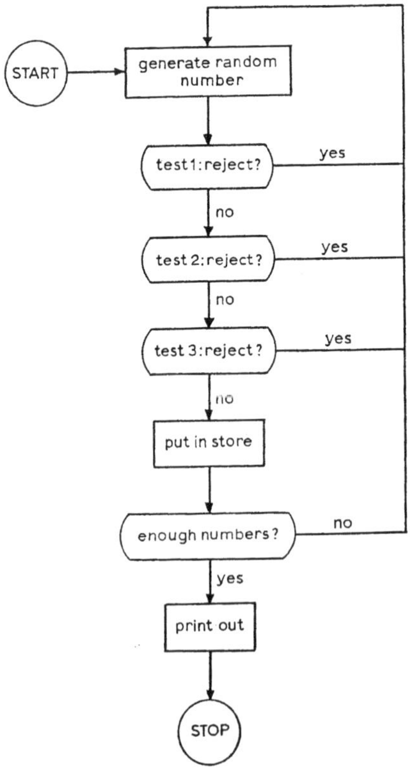

FIG. 17

The nature of the particular rules used determines the nature or 'style' of the composition. At the most general level such rules determine whether the piece is in the style of, for example, Gregorian chant, sonata form or traditional jazz—in each case the range of events which can occur at each stage is restricted by fairly precise and explicit rules. In principle further rules can be added to give the resulting music greater individuality (in the sense in which both Mozart and Beethoven may be said to have produced symphonies in the same genre, but with different styles). Further it would be nice to lay down specific rules to ensure that a composition which is technically correct and has a particular flavour is also aesthetically pleasing.

(Note that in composing by generating possibilities and then rejecting in accordance with ever stricter and more specific rules one is decreasing the original randomness of the material and introducing increasing order. In information theory terms one is decreasing the amount of information.)

In the Illiac Suite, Hiller and Isaacson have, by experimenting with different rules, been able to produce music in certain styles —thus they have produced music in the style of both sixteenth-century counterpoint and modern twelve-tone. They have also attempted to add further rules to increase the aesthetic acceptability of the product; for example, in certain parts of the last movement the probability of selection of each note was made to depend in certain ways on previous notes chosen and therefore the randomness of note production was decreased still further.

The composer/programmers of this suite have shown that it is possible to use a computer not only to produce melodies but also music which incorporates harmony and a variety of rhythms and dynamics. Since producing it they have concerned themselves increasingly with the possibility of discovering the rules for consistently producing aesthetically coherent and interesting music. Their main approach to this problem, a problem of the utmost complexity, has been to think in information-theory terms, and experiment with programs in which choices are made to depend at each stage on elaborate statistical considerations. This would seem to be a promising line of research and may well throw light in due course on the psychology of art.

Computer poetry has also been written but with nothing like the creative sophistication of computer music. A common technique is to get the computer to fit words from a vocabulary into pattern sentences. Here is an example produced at the Cambridge Language

Research Unit.[1] The computer is programmed to write poems in the form of Japanese haiku by being given a frame with slots for the words to go into. For each of the slots a list of words is available for the computer to choose between. The choice is random, or may be constrained by a system which relates the words to each other, e.g. if the choice for slot 5 is 'pools', then certain words in the list of words for slots 1, 2 and 3 are excluded. Such a frame is shown below.

All . . . (1) . . . in the (2)
I . . . (3) . . . (4) . . . (5) . . . in the (6)
. . . (7) . . . the . . . (8) . . . has (9)

Here are two examples of haiku written in this way:

all white in the buds
I flash snow peaks in the spring
bang the sun has fogged

all green in the leaves
I smell dark pools in the trees
crash the moon has fled

Here random computer selections are constrained externally, first by the individual lists of words provided, secondly by the structure of the frame, and thirdly, and more interestingly, by semantic selection. A large number of haiku can be generated by the same program which, however, can hardly be said to display much intelligence or creativity of its own; and what it does do could be done more conveniently outside the computer. A similar criticism could probably be made of most computer poetry programs up to the present.

As well as music and poetry programs, a large number of programs have been written in the attempt to produce visual patterns which are aesthetically pleasing. These patterns are often presented on a cathode ray tube, but other methods are also used including especially the use of a computer-controlled plotter, i.e. a moving pen which draws directly on paper. Techniques include translating mathematical expressions into graphical representations and often repeating them in various ways (e.g. drawing a curve or a shape and repeating it in different positions and/or different orientations),

[1] McKinnon Wood, Robin, and Masterman, Margaret, 'Computerized Japanese Haiku', in Reichardt, J. (Ed.), *Cybernetic Serendipity* (Studio International special issue, July 1968).

generating random information and then applying rules (e.g. generating dots in random positions and then applying rules to connect them up in certain ways), and starting with a picture (e.g. a photograph) and transforming and deforming it according to various rules (e.g. turning lines into shaded images or changing the shape of the whole picture). For the interested reader, many examples of computer fine art are given in Reichardt.[1] (If the camera has removed much of the point of representational art, it looks as if the computer is poised to take over some of non-representational art too, thus pushing the encroachment of machines into visual art still further.)

The first question that one would like to ask about all computer art—music, poetry, and visual art—is how far it succeeds at all in its own terms, in producing feelings of pleasure in the spectator. Is computer art 'art'? My own impression is that most of the products of computer-art programs up to the present have either been too random or too simple to be aesthetically satisfying; other people may well disagree with this. It is perhaps a little surprising that more attempts have not been made to measure people's evaluations of this form of machine art. Indeed, one could envisage a feedback situation with the responses of the spectator being continually fed into the computer directing it towards the production of something which was more satisfying—at least to that spectator.

One attempt which has been made to test the effects of a piece of computer art objectively is that of Michael Noll. Noll analysed an abstract picture by Piet Mondrian and programmed a computer to generate a series of random computer pictures with the same number of horizontal and vertical bars in the same area as Mondrian's picture. Reproductions of one of these computer pictures and Mondrian's picture were shown to 100 people. The two reproductions are shown in Fig. 18, the computer version being on the left. 72% thought the Mondrian was the picture produced by the computer, and 59% preferred the picture which had in fact been produced by the computer.[2]

If computer art *is* successful, it is possible to ask the next question, a question of more direct concern from the point of view of computer simulation. How far do computer programs to create art of all

[1] Reichardt, J. (Ed.), op. cit.

[2] Noll, A. Michael, 'Human or machine: a subjective comparison of Piet Mondrian's "Composition with Lines" (1917) and a computer-generated picture'. reprinted in Hogg, James (Ed.), *Psychology and the Visual Arts* (London, Penguin Books, 1969).

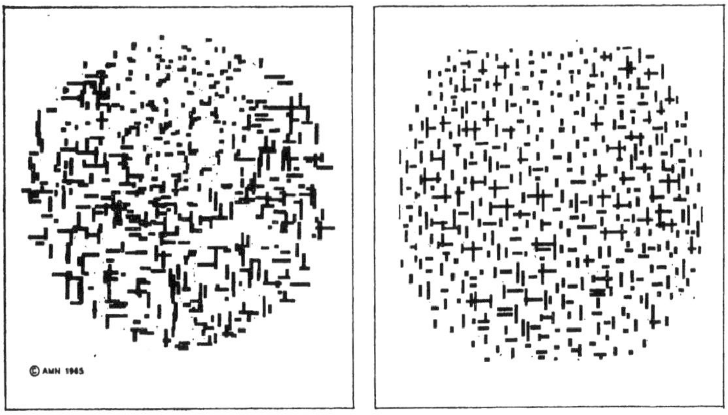

FIG. 18

kinds do so in the way in which human artists create works of art? Typically such programs involve two steps (and sometimes a continuing alternation of these two steps): first, possibilities are generated on a random basis and secondly a selection is made from these possibilities in accordance with certain rules. This process is exemplified in both the music and the poetry examples given. This is like the heuristic techniques we have come across elsewhere, e.g. Gelernter's use of a 'heuristic filter'. These computer programs may therefore lend weight to the idea that artistic creation is fundamentally no different from any other form of problem-solving. It could be argued that the best artists are those who can firstly generate the most random and the greatest number of possibilities and then can apply the most rigorous selectivity.

However, there are difficulties involved in assuming that human artistic creativity is of this sort. One might query, for example, whether it is possible for human thought ever to be truly random. Freud argued convincingly that every product of human thought is significant and in some sense meaningful, even errors. The designers and users of projective tests hold the same point of view.

Again, one might take Koestler's point of view that artistic thinking (and indeed all creative thinking) involves a process in which randomness may play only a subsidiary part: the process which he calls 'bisociation'.[1] By this Koestler means the deliberate

[1] Koestler, Arthur, *The Act of Creation* (London, Hutchinson, 1964).

bringing together of normally unassociated trains of thought. At least one computer program has been written for writing poetry which could be described as at least partly bisociative in nature.[1] This program combines and juxtaposes elements from three different passages (Michihito Hachiya's *Hiroshima Diary*, Paul Goldwin's *The Mystery of the Elevator* and Lao Tzu's *Tao Te Ching*). Here is an example of a stanza generated in this way:

> Hair between lips, they all return
> to their roots, in the blinding fireball
> I envisage their return, until he moves his fingers
> slowly, and although things flourish
> takes on the well known mushroom shape endeavouring
> to grasp while the multitude of things
> comes into being.

In a similar vein, Neisser[2] has argued that creative thinking involves multiple parallel processes interacting with each other and that if computers are to be programmed to think originally and creatively then parallel processing of the kind used in the Selfridge and Neisser pattern-recognition program described earlier in the chapter must be used in other kinds of problem-solving situations too.

What about the *response* to art? How far is it possible to simulate that? This question leads us to an argument which in different forms is frequently met with in the field of computer simulation: 'You could never create a computer which would be able to laugh, cry, be angry, blush, and enjoy going to the pictures.' In terms of this argument, aesthetic enjoyment, indeed any emotional response at all to any kind of stimulus, must for ever lie beyond the range of computers. Computers and humans are said to be, in this fundamental respect, different. And yet if the same kind of objective criteria are used as are used in behaviouristic psychology, or if Turing's test were to be applied to determine whether a system is emotional or not, there is no reason in principle why computers should not be programmed at any rate to display different kinds of *behaviour* which could be interpreted as emotional. Emotional behaviour will be considered in the context of computers in Chapter 8, *Personality*. If, however, one is referring in this argument against computer simulation to

[1] Balestrini, Nanni, 'Tape Mark I', in Reichardt, J. (Ed.), op. cit.
[2] Neisser, U., 'The multiplicity of thought', *Brit. J. Psychol.* (1963), **54**, 1–14, excerpt reprinted in Wason, P. C., and Johnson-Laird, P. N. (Eds.), *Thinking and Reasoning* (London, Penguin Books, 1968).

subjective aspects of emotions then genuine difficulties do arise; these difficulties will be examined in Chapter 9, *Consciousness*.

These questions in turn lead to another fundamental kind of question: why does artistic behaviour (on the part of both the artist and the spectator) occur at all? This question is given point by the argument that art would appear to be unnecessary in that it does not aid survival in any obvious way. Art—and indeed humour and sport and religion and many other human activities—although seeming to be important to us as humans, appears at first sight in a biological sense to be inessential. Why therefore do we humans expend so much energy and time in the pursuit of apparently biologically irrelevant goals? This kind of consideration, again, often leads people to the opinion that we are not simply survival machines and that therefore we cannot be explained in machine terms.

If this argument is correct, then the simulation of art by computer is trivial: the computer is creating art for *us*, according to *our* rules. Similarly, a computer playing chess is not *playing* the game in the sense in which we humans play—chess to the computer is no more a *game* than any other computation. It would make no difference to a computer whether it was directing a nuclear war or playing tick-tack-toe.

Although the argument in the last paragraph has obvious force when applied to current computer programs to create art and play games, it is far from clear that in principle computers could not, in effect, create computer art for other computers according to their own rules (such art quite possibly being not of the slightest aesthetic interest to us); nor is it clear that they could never play games in the playful way in which humans do. It may well prove to be the case that art and religion and many other supposedly inessential activities *do* in fact serve evolutionary purposes, perhaps in hitherto unsuspected ways, or that they are the inevitable by-product of those evolutionary processes that have led to man.[1] If this is the case, and if one day it is possible to create developing (i.e. self-complexing) and evolving computer systems, then it is also possible that, under certain conditions, behaviour functionally equivalent to behaviour like that involved in art, religion, humour and play will in some way emerge in computers too. Although no doubt it will be a very long time indeed before such an idea can be tested, it is perhaps unwise

[1] Ways in which this might have occurred are discussed most readably by Desmond Morris in his popular book *The Naked Ape* (London, Jonathan Cape, 1967).

meanwhile to deny categorically that such behaviour ever *could* emerge in computer or other man-made systems. And if it did it could provide a powerful explanation for the appearance of this kind of behaviour in man himself.

SELECTED REFERENCES

Hiller, L. A., and Isaacson, L. M., *Experimental Music* (New York, McGraw-Hill, 1959).

Nilsson, Nils J., *Learning Machines* (New York, McGraw-Hill Science series, 1965).

Reichardt, Jasia (Ed.), *Cybernetic Serendipity* (Studio International special issue, July 1968).

Rosenblatt, F., *Principles of Neurodynamics* (Washington D.C., Spartan Books, 1962).

Uhr, Leonard (Ed.), *Pattern Recognition* (New York, Wiley, 1966).

von Foerster, Heinz, and Beauchamp, James W. (Eds.), *Music by Computers* (New York, Wiley, 1969).

Wathen-Dunn, Weiant (Ed.), *Models for the Perception of Speech and Visual Form* (Massachusetts Institute of Technology Press, 1967).

7

LANGUAGE

The importance of language in normal human thinking is undoubted. Its possession serves to amplify intelligence to such an extent as to create effectively a qualitative difference between thinking in human beings and in all other animals. The communicative aspect of language is hardly of less importance. In this sense also its possession differentiates man from other animals, even those with comparatively elaborate signalling systems, and contributes to man's so-called 'superiority'. From the point of view of both the synthesis and the simulation of intelligent thinking and effective communication by computer, therefore, the development of computer linguistic abilities assumes great significance.

In general terms there are two ways in which computers may be used: (1) to carry out mathematical calculations on numerical data and (2) to process in various ways non-numerical data, i.e. symbols other than numbers, including the symbols involved in language. Although computers were originally constructed with the first purpose in mind, they have already come to be used increasingly for the second purpose. Thus business data processing, including information retrieval, involves the storage of much non-numerical information. The area of mechanical translation is obviously another one in which the computer processes language symbols, and occasionally computer-assisted instruction also involves the manipulation of natural language, e.g. in comparing a student's answer with a model answer in store. Of course all information is stored in computers in numerical form, but the numbers may be used as representations of other symbols and manipulated in ways which may be interpreted in a non-mathematical light. When this is done, a coding operation is carried out to convert symbols into numbers which can be operated on by the computer, and numbers can be decoded back into an output form which is appropriate for the user of the computer.

LIST PROCESSING

A technique which has been devised essentially to provide a convenient way of dealing with non-numerical information is that of *list processing*. List-processing languages (autocodes) have been used especially in programs dealing with natural language, as we shall see in this chapter (and also to some extent in Chapter 8).

In list processing each computer register contains two items of information: (1) the symbol being stored, and (2) the location of the register containing the next symbol. The second item of information is called the 'link'. So each symbol has associated with it the address of a location containing another symbol, and this new symbol in turn is associated with another address, and so on. In other words, the symbols held in the memory store take the form of *lists*, each symbol in turn directing the computer to the next symbol on the list.

To gain access to a list the computer must know the address of the first item, or 'head', of the list. Each list can include links to further lists, and in this way a complex structure can be built up. A structure of this kind, involving a main list together with sublists which may in turn lead to other sublists, is called a *list structure*.

The great advantage of this method of storing information is that the information does not need to be stored sequentially. Because of this, there is great flexibility in developing a list: a new piece of information can be added to the middle of a list, for example, without having to alter all the positions of the information in the second half of the list. This is done by putting the new information in any free register, changing the link so that it now refers to the register containing this new piece of information, and adding a link at the end of this new piece of information to the next item in the original list. Similarly, a whole new list could be inserted into the middle of another list. An 'available space' list is continually needed of registers which have not yet been used for storing symbols, for use when new information is to be incorporated into a list structure.

In conventional programming, operations like 'add' and 'subtract' are applied to stored numbers. In list-processing programs operations are applied to symbols, lists and list structures. The operations usually allowed for in list-processing languages include: comparing symbols, locating a symbol on a list, deleting a symbol from a list, combining two lists into one, and adding a symbol at the end of a list.

In the next section we shall look at several examples of programs which make use of list processing.

QUESTION-ANSWERING

One of the major uses of computers today, especially in industry, is for information retrieval. That is, the computer is used to store large quantities of information (e.g. concerning the staff, customers, throughput in the factory) and to retrieve particular sets of information (e.g. staff salaries, product delivery dates) when they are required. In many cases this is straightforward, while in others, especially where it is difficult to predict what information will be required and when, the problem is more difficult.

Question-answering, which is hardly used at all yet in industry or elsewhere, is an extension of information retrieval in the sense that the aim of a question-answering program is to retrieve information requested *in natural language*. Ideally, the reply to the question should also be in natural language, but most of the question-answering programs developed so far have been concerned with understanding rather than using natural languages—with linguistic analysis rather than linguistic synthesis. The aim of research in this field may be seen as mainly that of producing compilers which successfully treat natural language like an autocode and translate it into a form usable directly by the computer.

From the point of view of computer simulation, question-answering appears to represent the most direct attack on programming a computer to pass Turing's test.

Let us have a look at several representative programs in this field. A program written by Green, Wolf, Chomsky and Laughery[1] has as its aim no less than to get the computer to answer almost *any* question in natural English on a given subject. The subject chosen was that of baseball scores, i.e. the program answers questions posed in ordinary English about the dates, locations,

[1] Green, Bert F., Jr., Wolf, Alice K., Chomsky, Carol, and Laughery, Kenneth, 'Baseball: an automatic question answerer', in Feigenbaum and Feldman (Eds.), op. cit.

teams and scores of a set of baseball games during one year. This is of course a highly specific universe of discourse and one in which all the data can be tabulated in standard form in the computer memory store, using lists. But the strategies used by the authors of this program may be generalisable to a wide range of other subject-matters, and the program represents an important step forward in the computer understanding of natural language.

Some restrictions are in fact placed on input questions, including limiting questions to a single clause and prohibiting the use of structures implying relations like 'most' and 'highest'. But by-and-large the range of language structures acceptable to the program is wide, and it is believed that the restrictions could in future be removed in more elaborate programs based on the same principles.

Data on baseball games is organised in the memory store in a hierarchical list structure, the highest level consisting of months, each month being associated with a list of places where games were played, each place being associated with a list of games and the days on which they were played, and each game being associated with a list of teams and scores. Thus one might trace the following path through the data:

Month	=July
Place	=Boston
Day	= 7
Game serial no.	=96
Team=Red Sox, Score	= 5
Team=Yankees, Score	= 3

There is also in the memory store a dictionary which specifies for each important word that might be encountered its part of speech, its meaning, whether it is a question word, and whether it is part of an idiom—a contiguous set of words that functions as a unit. A similar dictionary is also provided for idioms. Some words, like 'the', 'did', and 'play' are simply disregarded by the program.

The program itself falls into two parts:

(1) *Linguistic routines*

First each word in the question is looked up in the dictionary. The result is that each word found in the dictionary is associated with the information found there.

Next a syntactic analysis is carried out. First, the question is bracketed into the noun phrases, and the prepositional and adverbial phrases, the verb being left unbracketed. (Prepositional and noun phrases are then also bracketed together.) For example: (How many games) did (the Yankees) play (in (July))? Then further syntactic decisions are made like whether the verb is active or passive and, if the former, which noun phrase is the subject and which the object.

This is followed by a content analysis which uses the syntactic analysis and the dictionary meanings of the words to set up a 'specification list'.

The dictionary meaning of a word might be as follows: the meaning of 'Red Sox' is 'Team = Red Sox' and the meaning of 'who?' is 'Team = ?' Or the meaning may specify a subroutine: for example, 'winning' has the meaning 'Subroutine A1 = Winning'. The latter subroutine has the result of attaching the modifier 'winning' to the appropriate noun.

The specification list represents the information contained in the question in the form of a list of the following kind. 'Where did the Red Sox play on July 7?' gives rise to:

Place = ?
Team = Red Sox
Month = July
Day = 7

Some specification lists involve modifications of attributes, e.g. 'What teams won 10 games in July?' yields, after the appropriate subroutine has been effected:

$\text{Team}\ (_{\text{winning}}) = ?$
$\text{Game}\ (_{\text{number of}}) = 10$
Month = July

(2) *Processing routines*

Processing involves a search routine that attempts in tracing through the data storage to find a path that achieves a match for all the pairs of terms on the specification list, except of course for the '?' term or the term 'each' in which case any value of the particular term in question is a match. For example, in dealing with the question above 'Where did the Red Sox play on July 7?' a match is required for (1) Month = July, (2) day = 7, and (3) Team = Red Sox. When these matches have been obtained, the term that is paired with 'Place' on the same path is the answer to the question.

More complicated questions, like 'In how many places did each team play in July?' involve much further computation—in this case generating a list of places for each team and then counting the list for each team.

In summary, then, the program converts question sentences

written in natural English into a specification list, matches this list with a path through the data in store discovering missing terms in the process, possibly carries out further computations, and finally prints out the answer to the original question.

The concept of *meaning* is crucial to any understanding of the ways in which human beings answer questions. This is a concept which is hard to capture, and involves processes which are difficult to reproduce in machine form. And yet for intelligent question-answering by computer it will sooner or later be essential. A program which attempts to tackle this problem, again for an extremely limited domain, is that written by Lindsay[1] using list processing.

The kinds of sentences that can be accepted by Lindsay's program are more restricted than in the baseball program and are limited to the Basic English vocabulary. But memory and recall in this system is more active and life-like than in the baseball question-answerer. The program is therefore partly about learning, thinking and the use of concepts as well as about information retrieval.

Lindsay points out that for the development of artificial intelligence, ways must be found of storing large amounts of detailed information while keeping the amount of memory storage capacity within realisable limits. He argues that to do this it is necessary to find efficient ways of storing implications of information. The idea is that humans achieve this in terms of cognitive structures which are pregnant with meaning and that it is necessary to simulate such structures. He points out that Gelernter's geometry theorem proving program (described on pp. 91–3) does just this by using diagrams which, although simple, contain large amounts of information which can be extracted by means of suitable calculations. Lindsay's aim is to do the same kind of thing, but with linguistic rather than geometric maps. (One is also faced with the same kind of problem in simulating biological development; here one must produce simple programs that each somehow contain within themselves enough information to build something far more complex.)

The area which Lindsay chooses for his first foray into this formidable problem is that of kinship relations. That is, his program is concerned with sentences about family relationships which involve concepts like 'father', 'sister', etc. Sentences about kinship relations are read into the computer which builds up a list structure of information, derived from these sentences, to represent

[1] Lindsay, Robert K., 'Inferential memory as the basis of machines which understand natural language', in Feigenbaum and Feldman (Eds.), op. cit.

family trees and their branches. Inferences can be drawn from this system of organised information to answer questions about who is related to whom and in what way. The point is that much of this information is not explicit but is contained implicitly in the mapping of relationships which is constructed by the computer itself.

The first part of the program is concerned with the syntactic analysis of input sentences containing information about family relationships. It parses each sentence by means of 'phrase structure rules' (see the section below on Chomsky) into its grammatical components.

The second part of the program deals with semantic analysis. First, a list of all nouns in the sentence is constructed including names used as possessive adjectives like 'Bill's'. Then subject-object combinations whose main verb is some form of 'to be' are discovered and the subject and object marked as equivalent, e.g. as in the sentence 'John is Mary's father'. Next, a search is carried out to see if any of the eight words which are available in Basic English to express kinship relations is in fact present. These eight words are 'father', 'mother', 'brother', 'sister', 'offspring', 'brother-in-law', 'sister-in-law', and 'married'. On the basis of all this information suitably analysed a list of relations is established, each item on the list consisting of two names and a relation word which connects them, as in the following:

John (father) Mary
Mary (mother) David

From such a list of relations, a family tree is constructed which in the computer store takes the form of a list structure. Here is a simple example:

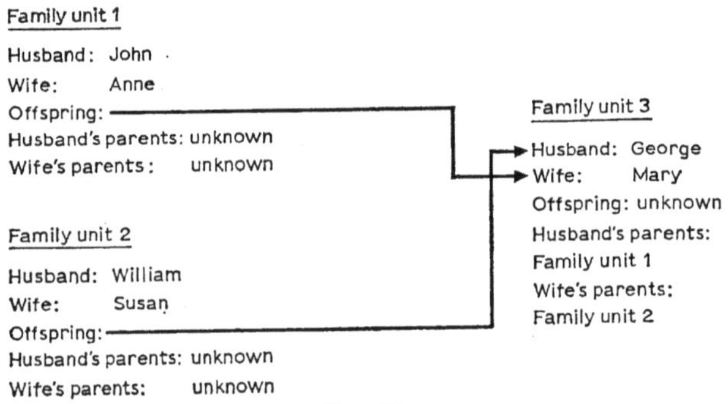

FIG. 19

A family tree of this kind continues to grow as sentence after sentence of information is added. Sometimes new information will establish new branches of the family, and sometimes it will allow blanks to be filled in the structure as it currently stands.

At certain stages it may be possible for the program to reduce the size of the tree and store its information in a more compact way. For example, if the computer has constructed trees representing the fact that *X* has offspring *A*, *B*, *C*, and *D* and that *Y* has offspring *E*, *F*, *G* and *H*, and it now receives as information input the fact that *B* and *H* are brothers, then the two structures can be collapsed into one representing a single family unit.

Having built a list structure of this kind, the computer can utilise semantic implications of a limited character in answering questions about relations. For example, if it is known that *A* is married to *B* and *C* is *A*'s sister, the computer can answer a question about the relation of *C* to *B* (i.e. that *C* is *B*'s sister-in-law) even though this information has not as such been read into the computer store. Similarly, if it is known that *A* and *B* are siblings and *C* is the father of *A*, the computer can work out, if so questioned, who is the father of *B*.

One criticism of this program might be that the mapping structure achieved is not all that compact and that the amount of new information which can be generated by the program itself is not all that great. This is in itself perhaps not too serious a criticism if the program is considered as a first step in the right direction. A more serious criticism might be that the program is too limited in scope to have any general significance, and is not generalisable to any other situations. That is, it could be argued that the strategies used could only be used with reference to family relations and that to deal with other situations quite different strategies would have to be used. Lindsay himself points out that connotative meaning in general presents a major problem to the computer programmer and one which he does no more than scratch the surface of. He also notes that many situations involve probabilistic relationships which make any attempt at simulation more complicated. One might add, too, that semantic relationships are not generally governed by clear-cut rules of the almost syntactic nature exemplified by the family relations situation.

However, at the very least Lindsay has drawn attention to what must be one of the most important and challenging areas for future research in computer simulation and artificial intelligence. Craik, one of the forerunners of cybernetics, argued that the human brain functions by building models of the world around it;[1] it is a form of model building which Lindsay himself is attempting to model. Indeed, modelling model-builders may turn out to be a generally fruitful approach to the simulation of human cognitive activity.

As in other fields which overlap artificial intelligence, progress —as measured by papers written if not by genuine achievements— is rapid. The two papers we have looked at are both examples of question-answering systems using list structures as their data bases. But other systems with other kinds of data bases have also been used.[2]

For example, work has been done on programs which retrieve information requested in natural language from continuous *natural-language texts.* A program written by Simmons[3] is a good example of this. Basically, what it does is to search through the text and pick out all the passages that each contain all the content words in the question. The chances are that using this simple rule the information required will come to light in one of the passages. Another program by Simmons illustrates how information can be retrieved from *graphic data.*[4] Based on the pattern-recognition work of Uhr and Vossler (see Chapter 6) it is able to make statements about displayed figures like 'the square is above, to the right of, and larger than the circle'. Yet another type of question-answering program is able to make *logical inferences* in answering questions. For example, Bobrow[5] has programmed a computer to accept algebraic problems written in a limited subset of English and to transform them into explicit equations which can be solved arithmetically.

It could be argued that each question-answering system programmed so far deals in a non-generalisable way with some very specific,

[1] Craik, Kenneth, *The Nature of Explanation* (Cambridge University Press, 1943, reprinted 1967).

[2] The classification of question-answering programmes in terms of data bases follows a review by Simmons which is the best review of this field known to the writer: Simmons, R. F., 'Answering english questions by computer: a survey', *Communications of the ACM* (1 January 1965), **8**.

[3] Simmons, Robert F., 'Synthex: toward computer synthesis of human language behaviour', in Borko (Ed.), op. cit.

[4] Simmons, Robert F., and Londe, D., 'Namer: a pattern recognition system for generating sentences about relations between line drawings', *Doc. TM-1798, System Development Corp.* (California, Santa Monica, March 1964), described in Simmons (1965), op. cit.

[5] Bobrow, D. G., Ph.D. thesis (MIT, 1964), described by Minsky, Marvin L., in 'Artificial intelligence', in *Information*, Ed., *Scientific American*, op. cit.

even trivial, part of natural language, and that general principles of question-answering have not yet begun to emerge. At the same time, to the observer with no knowledge of computers, the behaviour of some of these systems would no doubt seem to be surprisingly intelligent. How far real progress has been made in this field is difficult to determine at the present stage.

CONVERSATIONAL INTERACTION

Question-answering is really only one possible form of natural language interaction with a computer. It is one in which, typically, the computer output is no more than a few words in answer to a question, and in which all activity is instigated by the computer user. However, one can imagine a much more like-life computer use of language than this, in which the computer produces complete sentences as output and in which the computer can also ask questions and interact with the user in a less servile manner.

Here is an extract from a dialogue which actually occurred between a computer (*C*) and a person (*P*), interaction taking place through a typewriter. (For technical reasons the computer was unable to print out a question mark.)[1]

P: MEN ARE ALL ALIKE.
C: IN WHAT WAY
P: THEY'RE ALWAYS BUGGING US ABOUT SOMETHING OR OTHER.
C: CAN YOU THINK OF A SPECIFIC EXAMPLE
P: WELL, MY BOYFRIEND MADE ME COME HERE.
C: YOUR BOYFRIEND MADE YOU COME HERE
P: HE SAYS I'M DEPRESSED MUCH OF THE TIME.
C: I'M SORRY TO HEAR THAT YOU ARE DEPRESSED
P: IT'S TRUE. I AM UNHAPPY
C: DO YOU THINK COMING HERE WILL HELP YOU NOT TO BE UNHAPPY
P: I NEED SOME HELP, THAT MUCH SEEMS CERTAIN.
C: WHAT WOULD IT MEAN TO YOU IF YOU GOT SOME HELP
P: PERHAPS I COULD LEARN TO GET ALONG WITH MY MOTHER.
C: TELL ME MORE ABOUT YOUR FAMILY
P: MY MOTHER TAKES CARE OF ME.
C: WHO ELSE IN YOUR FAMILY TAKES CARE OF YOU
P: MY FATHER.
C: YOUR FATHER

[1] From Pepper, Charles E., 'The computer—big machine on campus', *Princeton University Quarterly* (summer 1966), no. 29.

P: YOU ARE LIKE MY FATHER IN SOME WAYS.
C: WHAT RESEMBLANCE DO YOU SEE
P: YOU ARE NOT VERY AGGRESSIVE BUT I THINK YOU DON'T WANT ME TO NOTICE THAT.
C: WHAT MAKES YOU THINK I AM NOT VERY AGGRESSIVE

The ingenious program underlying this dialogue, called ELIZA, was written by Joseph Weizenbaum at MIT. It utilises a collection of ways to find the most important key word in the input, break the sentence down according to a rule associated with that word, and construct a new sentence using a rule associated with the sentence decomposition rule. If it cannot find such a key word, it 'marks time'. Although the program is basically quite simple, it must surely be admitted there is a life-like quality about the computer's behaviour, at least for short periods. However, the lack of ability at drawing inferences from what it is told and of controlling the direction of conversation, means that the program is in effect simply a conversation-continuing device which has as one of its main objectives the concealment of its lack of understanding. To be more than this, as Weizenbaum himself points out,[1] it would need to be able to learn from people and then impart as well as receive information; it would also have to be given the power to model the person it is conversing with in order to make inferences about the person.

The particular form of Weizenbaum's program illustrated, was modelled on, and could be used for, the process of Rogerian 'client-centred' psychotherapy. Computers have so far not been used to any great extent for any type of psychotherapy. A practical field in which they have been used, however, is that of education.

As we saw in Chapter 2, in computer assisted instruction the computer typically guides the student towards some educational objective by means of a dialogue. This means that, unlike question-answering computers, the computer is essentially in control of the situation. In order to control the student successfully, the computer asks questions for diagnostic purposes and provides the student with information depending on answers to these questions. (In some cases the computer can also answer students' questions, and indeed as computer question-answering as a technique develops we may expect in the future that the dialogue between student and

[1] Weizenbaum, Joseph, 'A computer program for the study of natural language communication between man and machine', *Communications of the Association for Computing Machinery* (1966), **9**, 36–45.

computer will become better balanced and will more nearly resemble a tutorial situation in which both tutor and student ask each other questions.) Where the computer-student dialogue takes place using natural language, the computer's use of language may seem to be life-like. But the methods underlying this, at least at present, bear little resemblance to a human's methods of generating language: usually the computer selects pre-written and stored sentences, or even paragraphs, rather than constructing its own.

This confronts us with a fundamental question in the computer use of language. This question must be answered before the use of computers in a flexible and intelligent way, in practical situations like computer teaching, can be developed much further, and before the genuine computer simulation of human language behaviour can be achieved. The question is this: How can a computer build up a sentence from scratch to convey some intended meaning—and conversely how can it analyse a sentence so as to extract its meaning? Human beings, by means of a finite number of grammatical rules which relate to a finite number of words, are able to build up totally new sentences that may never have been used before and to do so for a potentially infinite number of sentences. They can also understand sentences they have never heard before and in principle do so for an infinite number of grammatically correct sentences. How this is done, and whether computers might be able to accomplish it, requires a more fundamental look at the nature of language itself.

A comparatively recent development in linguistics has in fact a direct bearing on this question. This development is due to Noam Chomsky of MIT who in 1957 published a book entitled *Syntactic Structures* which has had a profound influence on linguistics.[1]

THE RELEVANCE OF CHOMSKY

Chomsky's approach is highly consistent with computer simulation in that he believes that in order to understand language one must be able to write a precise and effective grammar (rather like a program) which can itself potentially generate all the grammatical sentences in a language and no ungrammatical sentences. In Chomsky's own terms, he argues that in order to understand linguistic *performance* one must understand linguistic *competence*.

[1] Chomsky, Noam, *Syntactic Structures* (The Hague, Mouton, 1957). A more recent work is Chomsky, Noam, *Aspects of the Theory of Syntax* (Massachusetts Institute of Technology Press, 1965).

First of all Chomsky demonstrates that English is not a finite state language; that is, that it cannot be generated by what is called a finite state grammar. Here is an illustration which represents a finite state grammar:

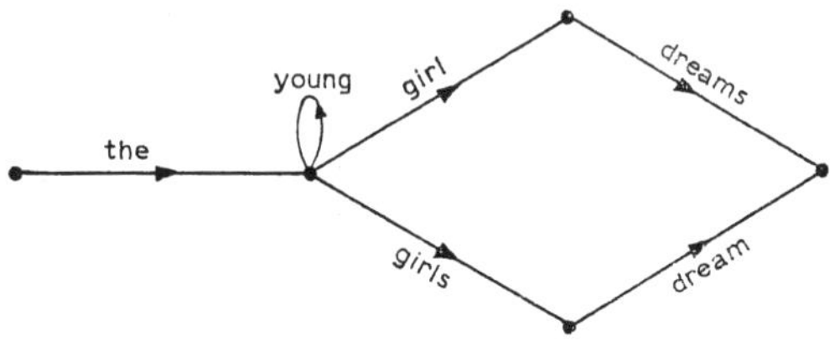

FIG. 20

This particular 'grammar' can produce a number of sentences. It switches from one state to the next by making choices sequentially as it moves from left to right, and in so doing produces a sentence, e.g. 'The girl dreams', 'The young girls dream', etc. The grammar—which can also be thought of as a language generating machine—is finite in the sense that it can be in any one of a finite number of states at a given time.

Although the grammar is finite state, it can produce an infinite number of different sentences because a new sentence can always be generated by going around the 'young' loop one more time in the generation of a sentence than has been done before. E.g. 'The young girl dreams', 'The young young girl dreams', 'The young young young girl dreams', etc. Thus a simple grammar of this type has, technically, one essential property that any grammar should have—it can generate an infinite number of possible sentences by means of a finite set of rules. Clearly, a fuller grammer of this kind would be an easy, if lengthy, process to programme on a computer.

Unfortunately, as Chomsky is able to prove rigorously, grammars of this kind are not able to produce the infinite complexity and variety of sentences of the natural language type. In fact it is in principle impossible to contruct a device of the kind illustrated above which will produce all and only the grammatical sentences of English (or, by implication, other natural languages). One reason for this is that sentences can be nested within each other. For example, a sentence may take the form 'If S_1, then S_2'. Sentences S_1 and S_2 may in turn have other sentences within them, e.g.

S_1 may be 'Either S_3, or S_4'. Dependency between words may have to stretch across many other (potentially infinitely many) words. In the example just given, the basic sentence involves a dependency between 'if' and 'then'—we cannot have 'or', say, in place of 'then'. And yet a number of sub-sentences may intervene. It can be demonstrated that a finite state grammar is inadequate to deal with such a situation.

The term 'finite state' may perhaps be misleading. After all, the human brain is finite and yet manages to use natural language; and as we have seen grammar must presumably be governed by a finite set of rules which, acting on a finite set of words, allow in principle an infinite number of sentences to be generated. The point is, however, that these rules, whatever form they take, cannot be of the type characterised by the diagram given above, to which the term 'finite state' is usually applied. Other kinds of rules are therefore required and Chomsky goes on to argue about the form that these must take. The new rules are also, of course, finite in number, but do not involve finite state processes in the technical sense used by linguists. These new rules are in principle just as amenable to computerisation, although more complex in form. What Chomsky in effect is saying is that natural language cannot be generated in the required way by a finite automaton like a network, but could be generated successfully by an infinite automaton like a Turing machine.

Chomsky proposes that two sorts of rules are required:

(1) *Re-writing rules*

These are the sort of rules used in what is called *phrase-structure* grammar. For example, a simple phrase-structure grammar might consist of the following rules:

(a) $S \rightarrow NP + VP$
(b) $NP \rightarrow T + N$
(c) $VP \rightarrow V + NP$
(d) $T \rightarrow$ the
(e) $N \rightarrow$ boy
(f) $V \rightarrow$ ate
(g) $N \rightarrow$ cake

where S stands for Sentence, NP for Noun Phrase, VP for Verb Phrase, V for verb and N for Noun. Each Rule $X \rightarrow Y$ is to be read as 're-write X as Y'. A sentence is derived by following these rules:

S
NP+*VP*
T+*N*+*VP*
T+*N*+*V*+*NP*
the+*N*+*V*+*NP*
the+boy+*V*+*NP*
the+boy+ate+*T*+*N*
the+boy+ate+the+*N*
the+boy+ate+the+cake

This process can also be represented in the form of a diagram:

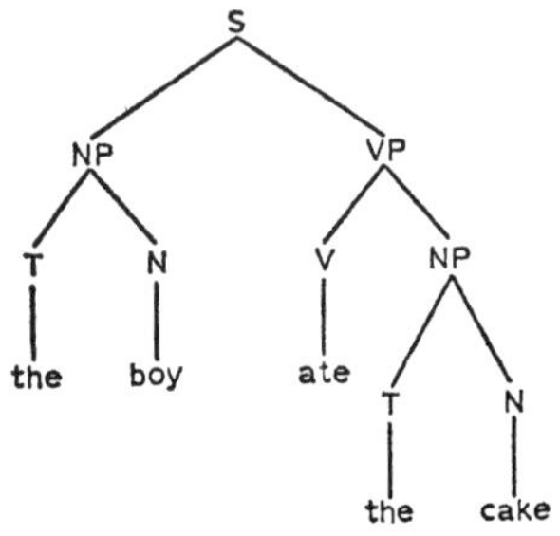

FIG. 21

(Obviously the process is only concerned with grammatical acceptability and the same rules could have produced 'the cake ate the boy'.)

With a phrase-structure grammar, then, unlike a finite state grammar, choices are not made sequentially along the sentence from start to finish; an overall plan for the whole sentence is chosen at the beginning and choices are made in terms of a resulting tree-like structure which derives from this plan.

The same process followed through in reverse results in a sentence being parsed.

However, Chomsky argues that a further kind of rule is also required:

(2) *Transformational rules*

Transformational rules may be applied to the output produced by rewrite rules in order to change the form of the sentence. For example, a sentence like 'The boy ate the cake' may be transformed instead into 'The cake was eaten by the boy' by applying a *passive* transformation, 'Did the boy eat the cake?' by a *question* transformation, 'The boy did not eat the cake' by a *negation* transformation, 'Was the cake eaten by the boy?' by a combination of passive and question transformations, and so on. Clearly defined rules in each case allow the correct transformation to be made.

This addition of transformation rules to a phrase-structure grammar is Chomsky's major contribution to linguistics. The resulting grammar is one which, Chomsky claims, is powerful enough to produce any grammatical English sentence of any complexity and in any form (interrogative, negative, etc.) and to do so in a way which is relatively economic and manageable.

Chomsky also shows that certain kinds of ambiguous statements which cannot be differentiated in terms of a phrase-structure grammar can be shown in terms of a transformational grammar to involve quite different meanings and could be derived by such a grammar from different roots. For example 'the shooting of the hunters' can mean two things depending on whether 'the hunters' are treated as subject or object. This is a case where two distinct transformational processes give rise to the same phrase.

Considerations of this kind lead Chomsky to argue that language has a *surface structure* which, roughly, consists of actual emitted sentences, and a *deep structure* which is the abstract grammatical relationships that underlie the surface structure. Thus two phrases like 'the shooting of the hunters' and 'the shooting of the hunters' may have the same surface structure but different deep structures. Conversely, the same deep structure can give rise to different surface structures, as in the sentences 'The boy hit the ball' and 'The ball was hit by the boy'. Using a phrase-structure grammar, one is confined to surface structures, but with a transformational grammar one can throw light on the relationship between deep and surface structures.

All this is of immense importance to the computer use of natural language. It is almost as if Chomsky's ideas have been put forward specifically for the use of computer programmers.[1] However, as Thorne[2] has pointed out, nearly all the work carried out so far in

[1] Chomsky's approach to linguistics can be regarded as part of a more general 'structuralist' movement across a number of subject areas, including especially anthropology. The assumptions and aims of those who call themselves 'structuralists' would appear to be not dissimilar to those of many of those working in the field of computer simulation.

[2] Thorne, J. P., 'Grammars and machines', reprinted in Oldfield, R. C., and Marshall, J. C. (Eds.), *Language* (London, Penguin Books, 1968).

computational linguistics is based on phrase-structure grammars and is therefore limited to the surface structure of language. One can hardly hope for more than restricted success in these terms for machine translation or for mechanical information retrieval using natural language. Thorne argues that in order to achieve success here it would be far better to try to model the way in which humans use natural language—after all it is unlikely that any system will be able to generate and analyse human sentences better than humans. To do this it looks as if such models would have to incorporate a transformational component. Chomsky's work therefore opens up a new terrain for computer simulation and artificial intelligence.[1]

It should be noted, however, that Chomsky's work is on syntactics and only marginally on semantics. For a sentence to be meaningful not only must it obey syntactical rules but it must also be consistent with certain semantic considerations. 'The cake ate the boy' and 'The boy ate the cake' are both syntactically correct, but only the latter is semantically appropriate. 'The green idea is fat' is also meaningful syntactically but not semantically. The whole topic of semantics and the relation of words to events and ideas is a complicated one. From the computer point of view, relevant work includes the work on pattern-recognition which we looked at in Chapter 6 and which involves configurations of input stimuli being related to internal representations, and the work on the learning of concepts mentioned in Chapter 4, as well as Lindsay's work described earlier in this chapter. Work specifically on this problem of computer semantics is being pursued at the Cambridge Language Research Unit.[2]

Three centuries ago Descartes used the observation that animals do not possess man's creative language ability as one argument in support of his assertion that animals are machines and humans are not. The development of the computer use of language, although at an elementary stage, suggests that language *can* be generated creatively by machine and that Descartes' argument was not well founded in this respect.

[1] To be accurate, it should also be added that Chomsky's theorising is sometimes, especially where he uses the concept 'mind', far from rigorous.

[2] Wilks, Yorick, 'Getting meaning into the machine', *New Society* (28 August 1969).

SELECTED REFERENCES

Bar-Hillel, Yehoshua, *Language and Information* (Massachusetts, Addison-Wesley, 1964).
Chomsky, Noam, *Syntactic Structures* (The Hague, Mouton, 1957).
Delavenay, Émile, *An Introduction to Machine Translation* (London, Thames and Hudson, 1960).
Foster, J. M., *List Processing* (London, MacDonald, 1967).
Garvin, Paul L. (Ed.), *Natural Language and the Computer* (New York, McGraw-Hill, 1963).
Lyons, John, *Introduction to Theoretical Linguistics* (Cambridge University Press, 1968).
Oldfield, R. C., and Marshall, J. C. (Eds.), *Language* (London, Penguin Books, 1968).

8

PERSONALITY

In the last four chapters we have been concerned with the simulation of different, although related, aspects of behaviour: learning, problem-solving, the recognition and creation of patterns, and the use of language. In this chapter we shall be concerned with the coordination of these abilities, through emotion and motivation, into cohesive, purposeful systems. In other words we shall be considering affective and conative as well as cognitive processes, and be asking about how they can all be integrated.

MODELS OF PERSONALITY

First of all, let us look at computer programs which have been written to simulate what can be termed 'personality' or aspccts of it. This is a field which is receiving increasing attention and a number of models have already been developed. But let us firstly consider one model in a little detail, as an example of work in this area. The model is that of John C. Loehlin, which he names 'Aldous' in honour of Aldous Huxley, the author of *Brave New World.*

Aldous brings together in the form of a simple model of personality a number of features of human behaviour: it recognises situations, reacts to them emotionally, and acts. It also has the possibility of learning and introspecting. But the main function of Aldous really consists in developing a set of attitudes towards the objects (or situations) in 'his' environment, these objects being identified as conjunctive combinations of a small number of properties. Input is read into the computer in the form of coded descriptions of these objects and output is printed out in the form of coded descriptions of responses.

The program reacts to an input in the following way:

(1) Relevant information in the computer memory is located which enables the input to be *recognised.* (Random errors on about 6% of trials are made by Aldous, this feature being deliberately programmed into the model, presumably to increase its realism.)

(2) The object recognised is then reacted to *emotionally* on the basis of (a) previous experience and (b) the model's current state. Three emotions are possible: 'love', 'anger' and 'fear'. The first of these may be described as positive and the second two as negative. Reaction may involve a combination of two or three emotions as well as a single emotion.

(3) An overt, behavioural *action* is selected and printed out. If the predominant emotion is that of love the action is that of approach. If the predominant emotion is that of anger the action is that of attack, and if of fear the action is that of withdrawal.

There is both an upper and a lower threshold for action. If emotion is below the lower threshold Aldous may be said to be indifferent and does not respond. If emotion is above the higher threshold Aldous may be said to be paralysed by an excess of emotion and therefore again does not respond overtly.

If two or three emotions are each above the lower threshold at the same time and approximately equal in intensity, then the model displays conflict behaviour.

When Aldous has reacted, another computer subroutine representing Aldous's environment determines the outcome of Aldous's action and Aldous may produce an emotional reaction to this consequence and also learn.

All this is summarised by the flow diagram on p.142.

Aldous is programmed to be able to recognise a finite number of objects—in the early experiments 1000. That is, each object is assigned a unique number in the range 0000–0999 and this specifies the address of its location in storage. Each of the three digits in the number is also said to represent a cognitive dimension, with ten values of each of the three dimensions, e.g. the number 309 would represent an object which had property 3 on the first dimension, 0 on the second, and 9 on the third.

For example, suppose the 1000 objects were taken to be animals of different kinds. Then the first digit might represent the species

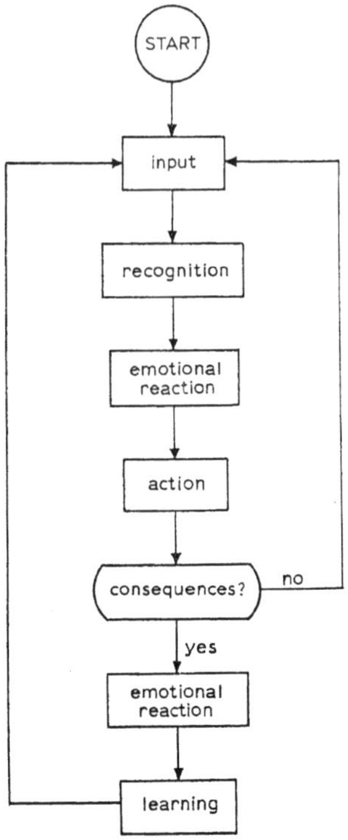

FIG. 22

of animal; 1 standing for human, 2 for cat, 3 for dog, etc. The second digit might represent the predominant colouring of the hair of the animal; 1 standing for white, 2 for black, 3 for brown, etc. The third digit might represent the age of the animal; 1 representing 0–1 years, 2 representing 1–5 years, 3 representing 5–10 years etc. So 132 would represent a brown-haired human aged between 1 and 5. The example is far-fetched and is used only to convey the idea. The principles that the model works on do not of course require us to interpret the numbers used as representing any particular objects in the real world.

Aldous's emotional attitude to any one of the 1000 objects it can recognise is represented by ten digits stored in a single computer word in the location specified by the address of that object. Here is an example of such a word:

Address	*Contents*			
514	0015	00	62	28

The first four digits of the word contain a count of the number of times the object has been encountered: in this case fifteen. The other six digits contain three values of two digits each representing the strength of Aldous's emotional attitude of love, fear and anger with respect to the object. In the example given Aldous is not at all fearful, very hostile and mildly attracted to the object in question.

As well as having emotional attitudes towards particular objects, Aldous also has attitudes towards types of objects. Using the example above we might say that not only does Aldous have attitudes towards brown-haired humans between the ages of 1 and 5 (132s) but also towards all brown-haired humans (13–s), all humans between 1 and 5 (1–2s), all brown-haired animals (–3–s) all humans (1– –s), etc. etc. Each of these more abstract higher order categories is represented at an additional location whose contents represent the number of previous encounters and the strength of the three emotions.

Each time Aldous has, say, a pleasant encounter with a particular object, such as 132, his emotional attitude to each of the related higher-order categories (e.g. all 1– –s, all –3–s, etc.) is also modified. But since change of attitude is programmed to be inversely proportional to the amount of previous experience with the object or type of object (more experience resulting in less change per each new experience), Aldous is likely to change his attitude less towards higher-order categories than towards objects themselves. This is because Aldous will normally have had more encounters with, say, humans (1– –s) than with brown-haired humans aged between 1 and 5 (132s).

This presence of attitudes toward higher-order categories allows the model to make emotional responses towards particular objects which have not been met with before. Aldous may not before have met a black-haired dog aged between five and ten but he may have developed emotional attitudes to black-haired animals and to dogs and these permit him to make an initial response to this particular novel object.

What happens when, as is typical, Aldous's emotions towards a particular (familiar or novel) object are mixed? In general the action which Aldous takes is determined in the following way. The relevant set of values of the three emotions from the memory store relating to this object are combined with the values of the three emotions from the previous emotional response (representing Aldous's current mood). Once a weighted combined value for each of the emotions has been computed they interact, the strongest emotion tending to weaken the others. The action then taken is determined by the following rules: if the strength of the strongest emotion is less than 2, no action: if 3–5, mild action of the appropriate kind (see above); if 6–8, strong action of the appropriate kind; if 9, paralysis. If the two strongest emotions are equal and above 2, conflict occurs.

The outcome of the action is determined, as we have seen, by a subroutine representing the environment. This outcome is in terms of three attributes—injury, frustration and satisfaction—corresponding to Aldous's emotions of fear, anger and love respectively. A fourth environmental attribute—power—represents the strength of the consequences. The subroutine also determines whether there are to be additional consequences: there would *not* be if, for example, Aldous withdrew from an object of low power but there *would* be if, for example, Aldous approached an object of greater power. If there are no further consequences the previous attitude in store is modified in that the frequency count has increased making the attitude more difficult to modify. If there *are* further consequences, these are translated into the corresponding emotions and the learning subroutine modifies the relevant attitudes in the permanent memory store accordingly.

Aldous may also introspect in the sense that information about his attitudes (to the last object, to the current object, or indeed to any specified object or higher-order type of object) may be retrieved by means of question inputs in appropriate form.

Two Aldouses may differ in their 'personality' for either of two reasons:

(1) Their experiences may be different, i.e. environmental outcomes may have differed and thus led to different attitudes. The order of presentation of objects may also have an effect on attitudes.

(2) Their 'innate' parameters may be different. A number of types of Aldous in this sense have been programmed by Loehlin and their behaviour observed: 'One version, called Abstract Aldous, places relatively heavy weight on higher-order memory classifications. Then there is Decisive Aldous, who acts strongly on slight emotion, and Hesitant Aldous, who acts only weakly on

strong emotion. And finally there are Radical and Conservative Aldouses, who differ from Standard Aldous in two parameters—the weight given to current mood and the rapidity of memory change—making Radical Aldous highly reactive to current conditions and Conservative Aldous more governed by his past.'[1]

What does one gain from such a model? So many arbitrary decisions have been made in both designing the overall structure of the model and in choosing particular parameters for it that one might argue that one gets out of it exactly what one puts into it and that Aldous helps little if at all in increasing one's understanding of human personality. However, the first models in any area of computer simulation are likely to show comparatively little returns for the effort involved—to seem in fact like setting up a printing press in order to write a letter. What a model such as Loehlin's does is to help to bring the behaviour we are trying to understand into focus and to clarify the nature of the problem.

From this model it becomes clear for example, as Loehlin himself points out, that there is a problem of information storage. The storage space needed by Aldous increases rapidly with any increase in the complexity of his world. Loehlin has worked out that with only 4 emotions, 9 cognitive dimensions (like age, hair colour, etc.) and 4 values per dimension, 9,765,620 memory storage spaces would be required. But human beings presumably have emotional attitudes to a large number of features of the world, and certainly more than 9. How therefore does the human nervous system cope with the complexity that is apparently involved? Some means other than that used by Aldous would seem to be involved. The question of the organisation of information storage is one that has not been attended to, to any great extent, by psychologists working in the field of attitudes. Aldous therefore puts the problems of the field in a new perspective.

Something else that should be said is that although Aldous is quite simple as a model, only a little complexity has to be added for the behaviour of this model to become difficult to predict and even unexpected, and in this sense one gets more out of the computer than one puts in (although of course unexpected behaviour would not be unexpected if one went to the great trouble of working out all the relevant details outside the computer). Thus when two Aldouses interact with each other, simulating a social psychological

[1] Loehlin, John C., *Computer Models of Personality* (New York, Random House, 1968), p. 40.

situation in which the input of one is the output of the other and *vice versa,* the behaviour of each may become difficult to predict.

For example when both Aldouses start off with fairly strong positive attitudes to each other, interaction at first (the 'honeymoon' phase) is almost wholly positive: affection increases, hostility and fear diminish. Then a period of 'quarrelling' occurs in which, intermittently, attacks and conflicts occur and relations generally worsen. Finally there is a recovery of positive affections.

In another interaction 'experiment', one Aldous was programmed to produce a positive output for any input ('Saint Aldous'), the other to be predominantly negative. The result was that the positive behaviour, far from making the second Aldous more positive, proved highly frustrating to it and caused it to become violently aggressive —so producing a situation not unknown in the supposedly more complex field of *human* behaviour.

Even a simple model such as Aldous may therefore produce complex and life-like behaviour under certain conditions. It is clear, however, that for further progress to be made Aldous would have to become more complex. In particular one would like to see added the possibility of Aldous planning rather than always reacting to the current situation and also the possibility of Aldous changing not only his attitudes but also the parameters (degree of weighting of current mood, minimum threshold for action, etc.) which govern the acquisition and change of attitudes.

A number of other models which may be classified as models of personality have also been developed, all of them more complex than Loehlin's. In particular, models have been programmed by Abelson and by Colby which involve mental mechanisms of a Freudian nature, and which manipulate symbols in the form of words and sentences.[1]

Abelson's model is written in a list-processing language and is really a model of Heider's balance theory. It reads in statements like 'Billy loves cats' and 'I throw rocks' and evaluates them in terms of its current belief system. Depending on how well it fits the system each statement is either accepted, rejected or modified. Accepted statements are added to the belief system which therefore develops over time, and this means that its evaluation of a given

[1] Abelson, Robert P., 'Computer simulation of "hot" cognition'; Colby, Kenneth Mark, 'Computer simulation of a neurotic process'; both in Tomkins, Silvan S., and Messik, Samuel, *Computer Simulation of Personality* (New York, Wiley, 1963). Both models are well described in Loehlin, John C., *Computer Models of Personality* (New York, Random House, 1968).

input statement may well be different at different times. Rejection occurs when a statement is deemed, in accordance with various criteria, to be incredible. Modification occurs when the constituents of a credible sentence are emotionally imbalanced as evaluated by the computer. For example, 'Billy' may have a current evaluation in the belief system of $-\cdot 50$ and 'loves cats' a current evaluation of $+\cdot 50$; the computer therefore must try to reduce the imbalance of the sentence 'Billy loves cats'. There are two ways in which it can reduce such an imbalance. Either it can use the mechanism of denial, in which case the sentence is simply made acceptable by negation ('Billy does not love cats') or the mechanism of rationalisation can be brought to bear. This is rather more complex but involves an attempt to construct an acceptable compound sentence in which the input sentence is embedded, e.g. 'Billy's cat loving is dishonest', where 'is dishonest' has a negative evaluation. Evaluation of subjects and predicates change every time a given subject and predicate are brought together during processing in that any discrepancy in their evaluations lead to a change in both evaluations so as to reduce the discrepancy slightly on each pairing.

Colby's program is also written (in its original form) in a list-processing language. It can be described as a model of the neurotic personality and is derived from psychoanalytic theory. If Abelson's model is an input model in the sense that it takes in and evaluates beliefs from its environment, Colby's model is primarily an output model in the sense that it starts off with a structure of beliefs which it 'thinks about', occasionally 'expressing' a belief by printing it out. Initially a belief is selected and a set of related beliefs identified. Each of these beliefs is then processed one by one. If no serious conflict exists between a belief and each of the others, it is printed out. If there is a conflict an attempt is made to modify the belief by means of a defence mechanism of which eight main types are available. If this succeeds the new transformed version of the belief is printed out. If not, another attempt is made at modification. Every time a failure to express a belief occurs, 'anxiety level' rises; conversely anxiety is lowered when a belief is expressed. If, after a series of failures to reduce conflict and express a belief, the anxiety level becomes too great and exceeds an upper threshold, then the whole topic is dropped and a new set of beliefs for processing is selected. Processing *can*, as in Abelson's model, be initiated by an input; in fact it is possible to simulate the psychotherapy situation by directing the 'thoughts' of the model towards particular beliefs and by doing so in such a way as to lower the anxiety level.

More recently, Colby *et al.*[1] have developed a program to conduct psychotherapeutic interviews along the lines of Weizenbaum's ELIZA (see Chapter 7). The intention of this is eventually to be able to gather information about a real patient which can be built into a computer model of the kind just described. This raises the attractive possibility of one day being able to discover from the model of a patient which psychotherapeutic strategy is most likely to achieve success and which strategies must be avoided. It need hardly be added, however, that such a day is still far off.

In the three models which we have considered in this section attitudes—that is, concepts or objects with associated emotional evaluations—have been used as the basic units.

The three models have also involved some kind of 'social' interaction—with the human computer user in the case of Colby's and Abelson's models and with other versions of the same model in Loehlin's case. They lead us therefore into the question of the simulation of social psychological situations. A model explicitly intended as a simulation of social behaviour is that of Gullahorn and Gullahorn[2] which is based on the theory of George Homans.[3] Homans' theory is ideal for computer representation in that it is stated precisely and elegantly in terms of five propositions derived from classical economics and reinforcement learning theory. These propositions are converted directly into a list-processing program which represents an individual in a social situation. A number of versions of this program, which the Gullahorns call HOMUNCULUS, are then set up to interact with each other. At first, two versions were programmed to interact together; in later work, three versions were used. Typically, each version starts with a set of pre-programmed attitudes and develops others during the course of interaction. Under appropriate conditions interaction patterns can emerge which indeed are not dissimilar in certain respects from what one might expect from human interaction.

There are a few other models of social processes, like that of Coe,[4] but on the whole this field is comparatively underdeveloped. There

[1] Colby, Kenneth Mark, Watt, James B., and Gilbert, John P., 'A computer method of psychotherapy', *Journal of Nervous and Mental Disease* (1966), **142**, 148–52.

[2] Gullahorn, John T., and Gullahorn, Jeanne E., 'A computer model of elementary social behavior', reprinted in Feigenbaum and Feldman (Eds.), op. cit.

[3] Homans, George C., *Social Behavior: Its Elementary Forms* (New York, Harcourt, Brace and World, 1961).

[4] Coe, Rodney M., 'Conflict, interference and aggression: computer simulation of a social process', *Behavioral Science* (April 1964), **9**, 2, 186–97.

are also computer models of large organisations[1] and of international relations.[2]

EMOTION AND MOTIVATION

The term 'emotion' was used a number of times in describing models of personality, and usually referred to some number in the memory store of the model which specified, depending on its location, the strength of some emotion labelled as, for example, 'love' or 'hate'. This seems a highly unsatisfactory way of thinking of emotion—as no more than a number in a particular place. One is forced therefore to consider more carefully what is meant by 'emotion' and whether it is possible to encompass it in computer terms.

There are, of course, two aspects of the emotions, and everyday language tends not to distinguish clearly between them. Firstly there is the conscious or subjective aspect—the actual feeling of pain or love or jealousy. Secondly there is emotion as something which is observable from the outside, either at the level of behaviour (like stamping one's foot) or at the physiological level (like increased rate of heart beat). It is the second aspect, the one which is more amenable to objective scientific investigation, which we shall be concerned with here. The question of the subjective aspect is, however, not being side-stepped and it will be confronted squarely in Chapter 9 when the whole question of consciousness is examined.

Emotion is closely related to motivation and this is recognised linguistically by the similarity of the two words themselves. We obviously want to consider motivation from an information-processing point of view as well as the emotions. If we attend to motivation first it will be easier to deal with emotionality afterwards.

As was argued in the chapter on cybernetics, there is nothing mystical about motivation and purpose. The old 'teleological' argument that purpose implies that the future is controlling the present and that therefore human behaviour cannot be explained in mechanistic terms has now been shown to be false: purpose can be described in the completely mechanistic terms of cybernetics. And a computer playing draughts may be just as purposeful as its human opponent.

[1] See, for example, Rome, Sydney C., and Rome, Beatrice K., 'Computer simulation toward a theory of large organisations', in Borko (Ed.), op. cit.
[2] See, for example, Benson, Oliver, 'Simulation of international relations and diplomacy', in Borko (Ed.), op. cit.

But there still seems to be some mystery. Thus one could plead: 'A system utilising negative feedback might be able to achieve some goal, but where does this goal come from? Humans choose their own goals, but computers and cybernetic devices have goals chosen for them.' While it is undoubtedly true that computers and cybernetic devices have goals chosen for them at a certain level, the same is also true of human beings. The overall biological goal of survival, for ourselves and also for our species, is programmed into us from birth. Presumably all the goals which we pursue derive more or less directly from this original survival goal in the same way in which a computer may generate its own subgoals (GPS is an excellent example of this) in order to achieve a goal determined by the computer user. Of course the relation between certain human activities (like art and religion) may be difficult to relate to the goal of survival, but there is no good biological reason to suppose that they do not.

The motivational system of human beings then can be regarded as consisting of a hierarchy of goals, the overall one being that of survival of the species. This gives rise to goals like the survival of oneself and the survival of one's family, these giving rise to subgoals like eating, exercising and copulating, these giving rise to sub-sub-goals like searching for food and cooking, these in turn giving rise to lower level goals like peeling potatoes, chopping them up, and putting them in a saucepan, and these giving rise to even lower level goals like grasping a potato and picking it up. Goals may sometimes conflict with each other, and the system may sometimes break down—after all, people sometimes commit suicide—but the motivational system, at least when functioning normally, must have a structure of this kind.

Each goal, at whatever level it is, may be pursued by means of the organism comparing its current state with respect to the goal to some representation of the goal and taking whatever (negative feedback or error actuated) activity appears to be required to reduce the difference between the current state and the goal. Miller, Galanter and Pribram[1] have proposed a term to refer to this mechanism: 'T-O-T-E', which stands for 'Test-Operate-Test-Exit'. This can be represented diagrammatically (see Fig 23).

The system continues to test and operate until the test (comparison with a representation of the desired state) is passed, when the system exits from the loop; e.g. if one wants to touch something, one in

[1] Miller, George A., Galanter, Eugene, and Pribram, Karl H., *Plans and the Structure of Behavior* (New York, Holt, Rinehart and Winston, 1960).

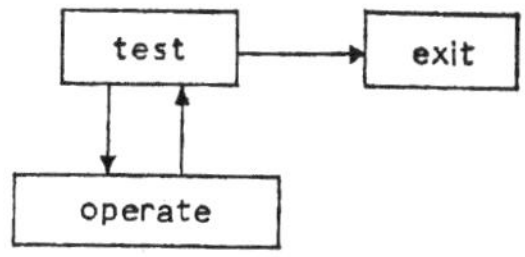

FIG. 23

effect alternates the operation of moving one's hand forward and testing until the test of feeling (or seeing) one's hand touch the object is satisfied. Then one exits and moves on to the next T-O-T-E unit.

Miller *et al.* further propose that this mechanism, rather than for example the reflex, should be regarded as the unit of behaviour. This would mean that motivation would be brought to the heart of psychology and the whole organism at all levels would be thought of as throbbing with purpose and directionality.

Consistent with the description of the hierarchical nature of the motivational system, T-O-T-E units are conceptualised as being built into hierarchies. For example, sets of T-O-T-E units would govern simple physical actions like touching things, grasping them, and pushing them; these could be organised into higher-level T-O-T-E units such as cooking a meal, and these activities organised in terms of even-higher-level goals such as entertaining friends. Miller *et al.* use the term *plan* to refer to a hierarchical organisation of T-O-T-E units.

Although behaviour is necessarily emitted in a temporal sequence of acts, these acts may be interpreted from the point of view being described as having been organised in terms of plans related to goals. (This reminds us of the idea of phrase-structure grammars, as described in Chapter 6, which organise temporal strings of words.)

There is no reason why computer programs should not be written in the same kind of way. Indeed, the situation just described is not unlike that of a program built up from sets of subroutines, especially where such subroutines involve as they often do loops which the computer goes round and round until some criterion tested within the loop is satisfied. In a slightly different way the relation between list-processing programs and plans, which can be thought of as lists of tests to perform, should be evident. And GPS is a program which demonstrates particularly clearly how a computer can function in terms of hierarchies of goals.

In the case of GPS, presumably just like the human nervous system, goal-seeking activity may involve the *generation* of goals: new goals are chosen or set up as part of the pursuit of a higher-level goal. Many of these subgoals may be essentially cognitive, e.g. to obtain a particular piece of information, to generate a pattern or to solve a problem. This view is thoroughly consistent with cybernetics and makes it clear that one of the criticisms of cybernetics —that it regards all behaviour as aimed towards restoring immediate physiological homeostasis—is without foundation.

Many goals require the integrated activity of the whole body for their achievement. Such goals must therefore be pursued one at a time if the organism is to be successful: if one attempts to copulate at the same time as hunting for food one is not likely to succeed very well in either activity. Similarly, other goals must be pursued individually because each requires the undivided attention of the individual: it is, for example, difficult to read, write and hold a conversation at the same time. Thus there must be some part of a system like the nervous system which acts as a controller by determining which goals to pursue in which order, at least for certain kinds of goals. At the level of the autonomic nervous system, of course, a large number of homeostatic goals are achieved concurrently—heart rate, respiration rate, speed of food digestion, etc. —but even here under certain conditions, like emergency, these various activities are coordinated so as, for example, to alert the whole body and prepare it for 'fight or flight'.

This may all seem obvious, but putting things in this way makes it easier to see that if there is nothing mysterious about motivation, there is nothing mysterious about emotional behaviour either. Thus one way in which emotions function is to act as a mechanism which interrupts the current goal-seeking behaviour and causes the controller to attend to a different goal. Sudden danger or noxious stimulation causes the organism to try to reduce such danger or stimulation as an immediate priority and to over-ride other goals. This may involve voluntary skeletal activity as well as the coordination of involuntary autonomic processes. Simon[1] has argued in some detail in the context of information-processing models that interruption mechanisms, having some of the properties usually ascribed to emotion, allow a system to respond to urgent needs in real time. It is clear that one could program a computer to behave in the same kind of way on the input of certain kinds of information. The function of an emotional subsystem of the kind described is an adaptive one which increases the chance of an organism surviving. But why is emotion sometimes apparently disruptive and maladap-

[1] Simon, Herbert A., 'Motivational and emotional controls of cognition', *Psychological Review* (1967), 74, 1, 29–39.

tive? Simon argues that what happens in such cases is that certain stimuli, if persistent as well as intense, continually interrupt any plan of behaviour to such an extent that no goal, including the goal of escaping such stimuli, can be pursued successfully.

Emotions, at least in a slightly broader sense of the term, may perhaps fulfil a function rather wider than that described by Simon. In particular, one could argue that they in some way exert a continuing influence over the controller in the choice it makes of goals to pursue in non-emergency as well as emergency situations. The evaluative weightings assigned to different strategies in a program like the draughts-playing program of Samuel could be interpreted as functionally analogous to emotional feelings we have in weighing up what to do in a problem situation which involves choice—and which determine which choice is finally made. In a similar way, the strengths of the 'emotions' attached to objects in the environment of Loehlin's Aldous determines how Aldous will in fact act.

No doubt, and not only if psychoanalysts are to be believed, the emotional system of human beings and its relation to the cognitive system is highly complicated. It will presumably be a long time before we understand the details of the functioning of the emotions. However, an information-processing approach may well help to unravel these details in a thorough and systematic way.

ARTIFICIAL LIFE

This chapter is concerned with integration. The models of personality described earlier showed a preliminary kind of integration, centred especially around the idea of attitudes and emotional evaluations, which to some extent relate perception, learning, motivation and the emotions.

A more direct approach to integration would be to produce computer models of the nervous system as a whole in which models such as those described in previous chapters on learning, pattern-recognition, problem-solving, and so on, could be combined as subroutines of a more comprehensive program.[1] Consistent with the argument of the last section, the controller of such a program would essentially choose goals to be pursued (by specified subroutines), some of them concurrently and others sequentially.

[1] For a further discussion of how this could be carried out, see George, F. H., 'Logic, language and the nervous system', in Oestreicher, Hans L., and Moore, Darrell R. (Eds.), *Cybernetic Problems in Bionics: Bionics Symposium 1966* (New York, Gordon and Breach, 1968).

To make the situation more meaningful and challenging as a simulation, we should want to provide the computer brain with some equivalent of a body—something to control other than itself. One way to do this would be to feed in inputs representing information from some imaginary 'body'. More realistically, we could arrange for the computer to control some real physical system with some of the characteristics of an organism including its own receptors and its own means of moving around and manipulating its environment. Manifestly we could not put the computer inside such a system, at least not at the present stage of computer technology, although at some time in the future computers might become small enough to be put inside another system the size of an animal. However, a computer could be made at the present stage of development to control some other device—simulating the body of an organism—by remote control. And in fact a device of just this kind which can move around on a trolley and explore and manipulate its environment has been built at Stanford Research Institute.[1] Another device with similar abilities is being developed in the Department of Machine Intelligence and Perception at the University of Edinburgh.[2] These devices represent the beginnings of the applied field of robotology.

The idea of a mobile device of the kind described leads us to an even more fundamental, if hypothetical, conception of the simulation of a behaving organism. Suppose we programmed into the computer the goal of ensuring the survival of the system it is controlling. In order to succeed with this it would also have to ensure its own survival. We should therefore want to program it with the overall goal of ensuring the survival of the whole 'brain-body' system of which it is a part. If we could arrange in some way (which is difficult to envisage at present) for the body to be equally essential for the brain, by providing it with its energy, protecting it from attack, obtaining information for it from the environment, and so on, the whole system would be the analogue of a complete living organism and would be entirely autonomous, at least while functioning successfully.[3]

This speculation takes us towards a science fiction world of the future and towards a field which has not yet developed but will no

[1] Rosen, C. A., 'Machines that act intelligently', in *Science Journal* (October 1968), special issue on *Machines like Men*, vol. 4, no. 10.
[2] Michie, Donald, 'Machines that play and plan', in *Science Journal*, ibid.
[3] One is inevitably reminded of the fictional computer HAL in the film *2001* based on Clarke, Arthur C., *2001, A Space Odyssey* (London, Hutchinson, 1968).

doubt one day do so somewhere along the road from Bionics to a fully-fledged Robotics. If a name is to be suggested for all this field, 'Autonomics'[1] might be most suitable—the construction of autonomous self-supporting systems or, more simply, artificial living systems. Back in 1748 La Mettrie said: 'The human body is a machine which winds its own springs.'[2] Autonomics would concern all artificial systems which 'wind their own springs' in some sense or another. It need hardly be said that such a study, if feasible, would have implications for psychology and biology, as well as having valuable practical applications.

Some rudimentary autonomic systems already exist in special environments, like Grey Walter's mechanical tortoises which in principle will continue to function until they finally wear out in the special environment which contains terminals where they can recharge their batteries.

To construct a reasonably small system which would extract energy directly from the natural environment like organisms do will obviously be much more difficult. However, developments in the biological sciences make it more likely all the time that such systems will soon be quite practicable. Indeed it has already been demonstrated by Kuhn[3] and Katchalsky[4] that it is possible to have a system which will simulate muscle by converting chemical energy directly into mechanical energy, and Katchalsky has in fact gone so far as to construct a mechano-chemical engineering device using collagen fibres which converts chemical energy directly into continuous rotary motion.

The whole topic of artificial life is of course highly speculative at the present stage and has taken us some way from the computer simulation of behaviour as such. But the possibilities are surely exciting enough to have warranted this brief excursion.

[1] The term 'Autonomics' has in fact previously been used by A. M. Uttley of the National Physical Laboratory to refer to systems which look after their own operations.

[2] La Mettrie, Julian Offray de, *Man a Machine* (1748), English trans. (La Salle, Illinois, Open Court Publishing Company, 1953), p. 93.

[3] Kuhn, Hans J., 'Machines that imitate muscles', *New Scientist* (2 September 1965).

[4] Aaron Katchalsky interviewed by Robin Clarke, 'Chemical engines', *Science Journal* (March 1966).

SELECTED REFERENCES

Deutsch, J. A., *The Structural Basis of Behaviour* (Cambridge University Press, 1960).
Galanter, Eugene, *Textbook of Elementary Psychology* (San Francisco, Holden-Day, 1966).
Guetzkow, Harold (Ed.), *Simulation in Social Science: Readings* (New Jersey, Prentice-Hall, 1962).
Loehlin, John C., *Computer Models of Personality* (New York, Random House, 1968).
Miller, George A., Galanter, Eugene, and Pribram, Karl H., *Plans and the Structure of Behavior* (New York, Holt, Rinehart and Winston, 1960).
Stanley-Jones, D. and K., *The Kybernetics of Natural Systems* (Oxford, Pergamon, 1960).
Tomkins, Silvan S., and Messick, Samuel (Eds.), *Computer Simulation of Personality* (New York, Wiley, 1963).

9

CONSCIOUSNESS

Many readers will no doubt have followed the mechanist argument thus far with a growing feeling of dissatisfaction. 'Certainly,' one might say, 'during the years ahead it is possible that, with increasing ingenuity, computers will be built which can carry out more and more of the functions of the human nervous system and even improve on them in certain respects. But there is something that a computer will never, in principle, be able to achieve, and this is *self-awareness*. This is what, in the last analysis, will always differentiate between a computer and a human being. A computer might be able to think, but it cannot know that it is thinking.' The claim being made here, then, is that the existence of self-awareness in human beings constitutes a final and crucial limitation to the analogy between computers and man.

If we take the argument in its simplest form we can easily refute it. Thus we could write a program including a subroutine for inspecting the rest of the program. We could then say that this self-inspecting process involved a form of self-awareness. Loehlin's 'Aldous program' described in Chapter 8 would be an example of an introspecting program of this kind. Again, use of an executive program in time-sharing (as described in Chapter 3) might be cited as a widely found example of machine self-awareness of this type. Should it be objected that in these examples the inspection program was not inspecting continuously but only in alternation with the other program or programs, it could be pointed out that use of a simultaneous rather than the much more common sequential computer, or the use of two or more computers combined into a computer complex, could overcome this objection.

However, this would probably be to mistake the point of the criticism which could be restated more strongly as 'computers are not, and cannot be made to be, conscious'. The term 'conscious' here is being used to refer not to the focus of attention, or wakefulness in a physiological sense, or volition; it is being used to refer specifically to one thing: subjective experience. This brings us up against the mind-body problem which is probably the most intriguing and intractable problem with which scientists are faced: What is consciousness and what is its relation to the brain and to the body? Only when we know the answer to this question (or indeed whether the question can be properly asked at all) can we face the question of whether a computer could or could not be said to be conscious.

THE MIND-BODY PROBLEM

Let us look briefly at the history of the mind-body (or 'mind-brain') problem and solutions which have been proposed to it. On the whole they fall into two broad categories: those in which mind and body (including especially the brain) are seen as different in some fundamental way—dualist theories—and those in which they are not.

The dualist position can be traced back a long way, but it finds its best-known and classic exposition in the work of Descartes. He formulated an attitude to the problem which has had a continuing influence on Western thought—philosophical, scientific and religious —and which has even become embedded in everyday 'commonsense'.

According to Descartes there are two kinds of entities in the universe: mind and matter. They are distinguished in the following way: matter has extension in space and obeys the physical laws of mechanics whereas mind has neither of these attributes. The human body is said to be composed of matter but acts upon and is in turn acted upon by mind (or 'the soul'). As we saw earlier (p. 15) Descartes even specified a locus for this interaction in the pineal gland. Thus in Descartes' view there are not only two kinds of entity, but in the human being these two entities interact; so Descartes may be described as not only *dualist* but also as *interactionist*. We can summarise this doctrine by the following diagram:

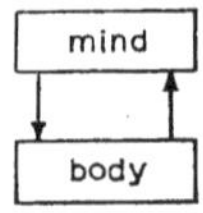

FIG. 24

In these terms the mind can, through its function of volition, cause the body to act in certain ways, e.g. the desire to stretch the arm can cause the arm to be in fact stretched. Similarly the body acts on the mind, e.g. perception of the movement of the arm is relayed to the mind by the body. So the mind acts as a controller within the body or, as Gilbert Ryle has disparagingly put it, as 'a ghost in the machine'.[1] Ryle also points out that this dualism allowed Descartes, like others since then, to maintain both a religious and a scientific viewpoint: 'As a man of scientific genius he could not but endorse the claims of mechanics, yet as a religious and moral man he could not accept . . . the discouraging rider to those claims, namely that human nature differs only in degree of complexity from clockwork.'[2]

Descartes' is still very much the 'commonsense' point of view on the relation of mind and body. However, to the scientist and the philosopher crucial difficulties are involved in this viewpoint. The main one is that if mind and matter are, as Descartes claims, entirely different stuffs obeying entirely different laws, how can they possibly interact? A subjective 'wish' or a 'purpose' can no more hit a golf ball 200 yards than they can cause the hands and arms of the material body to clutch a golf club and do the same thing. A wish is a mental phenomenon, a golf stroke is a physical phenomenon.

A second dualist position, and one which gets around the difficulty inherent in the interactionist position, is that described by the term *parallel function*: mind and matter do not really interact at all, they only appear to interact. But why should they appear to interact and why should the mind appear to control the body? The answer proposed by this school of thought was that there was a 'pre-established harmony' (this term was introduced by Leibnitz) which brought about this continuous and precise correspondence or parallel function between mind and body. That is, mind and body are like two clocks which both keep perfect time. Each clock is completely independent of the other clock, but to a naive observer it might appear that the hands of the one cause the movement of the hands of the other, or *vice versa*. This argument was first put forward by Geulincx, a disciple of Descartes and strongly influenced the views of Leibnitz. It can perhaps be represented diagramatically as in the way shown in Fig. 25.

The philosophy of parallel function is difficult to find fault with if one accepts dualism although it involves the notion of determinism,

[1] Ryle, G., *The Concept of Mind* (London, Hutchinson, 1949; Penguin Books, 1963).
[2] Ryle, G., op. cit., Penguin edn., p. 20.

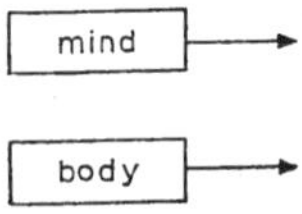

FIG. 25

which is difficult for many people, especially those of a religious disposition, to accept. Perhaps the main objection to it is, as Bertrand Russell has said, simply that it is very odd.[1]

A third dualist position which is still respectable in biology and was proposed by the great Victorian biologist T. H. Huxley is that of *epiphenomenalism*. This postulates action in one direction and one direction only: consciousness is regarded as a by-product of certain physical and chemical processes in the nervous system. The situation can be likened to a set of dials connected into a machine: the positions of the dials are caused by various aspects of the machine's functioning, but they do not themselves influence the machine. This idea can be represented by the following diagram:

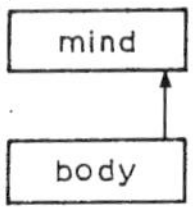

FIG. 26

That is to say, the body and, more specifically, the brain, function in accordance with physical laws and a by-product (which is admittedly puzzling) of some of this functioning is consciousness. If we knew enough about the neurophysiology of consciousness, we should be able to compile a dictionary of brain-consciousness correspondences in such a way that for any given feature of brain activity we should be able to look up the corresponding mental events and *vice versa*. In these terms there are no laws of mind, but mental phenomena are lawful because of their association with the brain whose activity *is* governed by physical laws. But part of the problem which Descartes faced still remains: is the conversion of brain to conscious activity a causal one, and if so, how can such causation be explained and if not what form of relation is it?

Of those viewpoints which consist of the rejection of dualism there are a number of varieties. For example, in the history of Western philosophy we find the opposing traditions of *idealism*

[1] Russell, B., *History of Western Philosophy* (London, Allen and Unwin, 1946), p. 584.

and its insistence on the reduction of matter to mind and of *materialism* with its reduction of mind to matter. If names are to be mentioned, Bishop Berkeley should be mentioned in connection with idealism and Hobbes in connection with materialism. In either case the problem of the relation of mental to physical events is by-passed either by the belief that we can only know about mental events (and in its extreme form that only mental events exist) or that we can only know about physical/material events (and in its extreme form that only material events exist). Interestingly enough we find something of this same opposition in modern psychology between Phenomenology and Behaviourism.

Not only are there theories which reduce mind to matter or matter to mind but there are theories which reduce both mind and matter to some common third term. For example, Spinoza regarded both mind and matter as aspects of God. More recently Bertrand Russell,[1] following William James, has argued that the material of which the world is made is neither mind nor matter but something anterior to both. This is called the doctrine of *neutral monism*. Again, there is the idea, sometimes referred to as *parallelism*,[2] that mind and matter are simply different aspects of the same process.

A large group of current theories argue that dualism is due to conceptual confusion and the misuse of language. This view of the mind-body problem as a pseudo-problem is of course consistent with the whole temper of modern analytical philosophy. According to it, all we have to do is to clarify our concepts or use language correctly and the problem will disappear. Thus there is really only one set of events involved, for example, in thinking or in volition but we tend to talk about this set of events in different ways related to different aspects of these events and this, unless we are careful, leads us to think in a dualist fashion. Among others who have argued essentially in this way, although differing in their views as to the exact nature of the mind-body confusion, can be listed Wittgenstein,[3] Carnap,[4] Ryle[5] and Strawson.[6]

[1] Russell, B., *The Analysis of Mind* (London, Allen and Unwin, 1921).
[2] For example this term is used in this sense in a number of the papers in *Dimensions of Mind*, Hook, Sidney, Ed. (New York, Collier Books, 1961).
[3] Wittgenstein, L., *Philosophical Investigations* (Oxford, Blackwell, 1953).
[4] Carnap, Rudolf, 'Psychology in physical language', in Ayer, A. J. (Ed.), *Logical Positivism* (Glencoe, Illinois, The Free Press, 1959), pp. 165–98.
[5] Ryle, G., op. cit.
[6] Strawson, P. F., *Individuals, an Essay in Descriptive Metaphysics* (London, Methuen, 1959).

For instance, Ryle argues that the concept of mind is based on what he calls a 'category mistake'. He gives an example of a foreign visitor being shown around the University of Oxford. Having been shown all the separate buildings the visitor asks 'But where is the University?', as if the University was just another building. In fact the University is 'the way in which all that he has already seen is organised',[1] and therefore is in a different category from the buildings of the University. Similarly, Ryle argues, to postulate the existence of mind in the same way in which one might postulate the existence of matter is to commit a category mistake because it implies that mind and matter are simply different kinds of 'things' or 'processes' whereas mind is not a thing but refers to dispositions to behave in various ways. So to say that 'there exist minds and there exist bodies' is rather like saying 'three things are now rising, namely the tide, hopes and the average age of death'.[2] In both sentences a single word—'exists' in the first and 'rising' in the second—is used in a set of different contexts which suggest different meanings for the word and the result is effectively that neither sentence makes good sense.

VIABILITY OF DUALISM

If, as we have just seen, philosophers have tended in this century to reject dualism, neurophysiologists have tended to accept it and puzzle over its nature. Among neurophysiologists and neuroanatomists who have discussed mind within a dualist frame of reference are Sir Charles Sherrington,[3] Lord Adrian,[4] Sir Wilfred le Gros Clark,[5] Dr Wilder Penfield,[6] Sir John Eccles[7] and Sir Russell Brain. (If nobility of the protagonists was anything to go by the issue would have been settled long ago.) The last mentioned has especially taken philosophers like Ryle to task for their belief that 'to find out the nature of mind, all one has to do is to sit in one's study

[1] Ryle, op. cit., p. 18.
[2] ibid., p. 24.
[3] Sherrington, Sir Charles, *Man on his Nature* (London, Penguin Books, 1955).
[4] Adrian, E. D., *The Physical Background of Perception*, The Waynflete Lectures (New York, Oxford University Press, 1946).
[5] Clark, W. E. le Gros, 'The structure of the brain and the process of thinking', in Laslett, Peter (Ed.), *The Physical Basis of Mind* (Oxford, Blackwell, 1950).
[6] Penfield, Wilder, 'Some observations on the functional organisation of the human brain', *Proc. Am. Philos. Soc.* (1954), XCVIII, 293–7.
[7] Eccles, J. C., *The Brain and the Unity of Conscious Experience* (Cambridge University Press, 1965).

and discuss the terms which are habitually used to describe activities defined as mental'.[1]

At this stage, I should like to state my own position on this difficult question. (The reader is warned that what follows in this and the next section of this chapter is a personal viewpoint; other points of view may be found in the selected references at the end of this chapter.) I find myself more in sympathy with the neurophysiological tradition of thought than with that of the analytical philosophers who treat the mind-body problem as a pseudo-problem. Consider a living human brain. At a given time a particular set of electro-chemical events is taking place in it. At the same time the person who owns (or 'is') the brain is having a particular conscious experience corresponding in some way to these events. He may be thinking for example of a picnic he once went on. The subjective, conscious, images of the picnic and the pattern of electro-chemical events which correspond to these images in the cortex are in some sense entirely different. (It should be clear that events can correspond with each other without being the same—for example a slide corresponds with the image which it projects onto a screen but is different from it.) Similarly, perception of the colour green is in some way quite different from the related neural activity, the very real pain one feels on being kicked on the shin is in some obvious way something other than the corresponding physiological processes, and the feeling of an emotion like love is not the same as the activity of hormones and the autonomic and nervous processes which underlie the emotion. In short, a subjectively experienced image or feeling or emotion is totally different from the (in principle) objectively observable neural and other physiological activity which relates to it.

It seems to me perverse to claim that this duality, which is something of such *a priori* extra-linguistic self-evidence, could be a linguistic muddle. If one was willing to go to extremes to demonstrate this duality to a sceptic, and to do so without recourse to language and its inherent dangers, one could do so in the following way. Strap the sceptic in question to an operating table, expose his cortex surgically, set up a mirror arrangement so that he can see this exposed area of his brain, and stimulate various points in this exposed area using an electrode in the manner of Wilder Penfield[2].

[1] Brain, W. Russell, *Mind, Perception and Science* (Oxford, Basil Blackwell, 1951), p. 80.

[2] Penfield, Wilder, and Roberts, Lamar, *Speech and Brain Mechanisms* (Princeton University Press, 1959).

This would, if suitable points were chosen, result in subjectively experienced sensations of some kind. (Ideally, and this may be possible one day, the individual should see his cortex actually functioning and not just its stimulation; but the point is clear enough that there is a physical process ongoing in the cortex corresponding to subjective experience.) It will then be clear to him, without needing language to express it, that the sight of the cortical stimulation and the subjective conscious experience, although related, are in some way different—that in fact they form a duality. Such a duality raises a number of problems and the problems are not all due to linguistic incompetence. Of course these problems can be avoided by denying dualism, but this would be no more satisfactory than to deny poverty if one was a politician in a backward country.

Perhaps the main problems posed by dualism are these: What is the nature of the conversion from brain to conscious processes? Why do conscious processes exist at all in a world which is apparently governed by the laws of natural science? Why are some brain processes related to consciousness while others—for example during sleep or concussion—are not?

It might be argued that parallelism, the aspect theory which says that conscious and brain processes are simply two aspects of the same set of events, would still be a tenable form of non-dualism. This would certainly provide a possible solution to the first problem posed in the paragraph above. But it would provide no solution to the other two problems, which could indeed be re-stated in terms consistent with this form of aspect theory. Thus: Why do conscious aspects of brain processes occur at all in a world which is apparently governed by the laws of natural science? Why do some brain processes have conscious aspects and not others? It would appear then that an aspect theory of this type is really a mild form of dualism, and in some respects is similar to epiphenomenalism.[1] It is also a highly defensible and attractive position.

At the same time, even if we must accept dualism in some form or another, this does not mean that we must accept interactionism. The argument that we should accept interactionism because of our subjective feelings that our minds control our bodies can be discounted since this would be expected on the basis of parallelism or epiphenomenalism as well. And teleological arguments to the effect that the concept of a controlling mind is logically necessary to explain purposeful behaviour are also unfounded if, as has been

[1] See, for example, the paper by Herbert Feigl entitled 'Mind-body not a pseudo-problem', in Hook (Ed.), op. cit.

suggested in earlier chapters, negative feedback is introduced as an explanatory concept. Meanwhile it involves fewer assumptions to adopt the working hypothesis that we can explain behaviour without recourse to an interacting—i.e. active and controlling—consciousness.

THE MIND-MACHINE PROBLEM

We have been looking at the mind-machine problem in order to try to become clearer as to the nature of consciousness before attempting to answer the question as to whether computers could be conscious. The main conclusions reached were that interactionism is at present an unnecessary hypothesis (and one which is inconsistent with the spirit of cybernetics in its attempt to understand organismic behaviour), but that dualism of some kind—perhaps in a mild form as in parallelism—must be accepted.[1] The fundamental nature of consciousness, however, remains a total mystery for science.

If we can distinguish meaningfully between consciousness and non-consciousness in ourselves, as we do for example when we talk about the experience of going under an anaesthetic, then it would seem to be meaningful to ask whether another system is conscious or not at a given time, or whether it could ever be conscious. This we do when we ask whether a computer is, or could be, conscious or not. If desired, this question could be rephrased in parallelist terms as: Is there, or could there be, a conscious *aspect* of thinking activities in computers?

In fact, the development of computers really brings up the mind-body problem in a new form. But this time instead of dealing with a system (the human being) which common sense tells us has a mind or consciousness, we have a system (computer) which common sense tells us does not.

I do not intend to try to complete the computer-human analogy of previous chapters by arguing that a thinking computer is in fact conscious. But I would argue that it is difficult to reject the idea of machine-consciousness out of hand, and that whatever attitude we take on it we have to face serious difficulties which may lead us to re-examine some of our assumptions.

[1] As far as cybernetics is concerned, it has been argued by some, like Sluckin, that cybernetics is anti-dualist. Others, like Ashby, believe that cybernetics is in principle neutral on the issue. See Sluckin, W., *Minds and Machines* (London, Penguin Books, 1954); Ashby, W. Ross, 'What is mind? Objective and subjective aspects in cybernetics', in Scher, Jordan (Ed.), *Theories of the Mind* (New York, Macmillan, 1962), pp. 305–13.

It might be pointed out, for example, that in judging whether some other organism has consciousness, or can feel pain, we normally allow our point of view to depend solely on the ability of the organism in question to communicate with us. Thus if we stick a knife into another human being we are willing to believe on the basis of the verbal and other information that he gives us that he is in pain. If we stick a knife into a pig we also believe, on the basis of subsequent squeals, etc., that it feels pain, although we are less sure about this. If we stick a knife into a fish we are less sure again. And if we stick a knife into a tree we are fairly sure that the tree does *not* feel pain. If we stick a knife into a lump of clay we feel certain it does not feel pain. So lack of communication usually implies a lack of consciousness. This might lead us to argue, as Hook has done, that: 'Our conclusion that machines have feelings —depends upon precisely the same set of considerations which lead us to the belief that other human beings have feelings. The exact point at which we conclude that objects hitherto regarded as nonhuman and treated as devoid of feelings have acquired them depends upon complex considerations, all reducible in the end to whether they look like and behave like other people we know.'[1] If this is true, then common sense would tell us that a computer programmed to pass Turing's test would also be conscious. Or if eventually an android[2] was built, we should have to conclude that it too possessed consciousness. To put this argument at its mildest: it is not completely unreasonable, or even inconsistent with common sense, to believe that a complex thinking computer might possess consciousness. Of course such a computer would not be 'alive', but as we have seen the concept of 'living' is not as useful or clear-cut a concept as was once thought. And to plead that something must be alive to possess consciousness is simply to beg the question.

Of course, it would be possible to argue that the criterion we should use to decide whether a system feels pain when we stick a knife in it is not the ability of that system to communicate with us, but the degree of judged similarity between ourselves and that system. Thus we would be justified in believing that a pig felt pain because pigs possess nervous systems not unlike our own. On the other hand, lumps of clay, as far as I am aware, do not. However, this too leads us into difficulties as we shall now see.

If we were to argue that the functioning of the nervous systems

[1] Hook, Sidney, 'A pragmatic note', in Hook (Ed.), *Dimensions of Mind,* op. cit.
[2] You will recall that this is a robot which is indistinguishable from a human being.

of, say, mammals, could be accompanied by conscious processes, but not that of any other system, then we should have to define what the crucial difference between mammalian nervous systems and all other systems was which was responsible for consciousness in the one and not in the others. We could not say that it was due simply to the organic nature of the mammalian nervous system, for then we should have to allow consciousness in plants, organic compounds, toes, noses, body cells, etc. We should also have to admit that computers made of organic materials (which as we have seen is not inconceivable in the future) were conscious. If the defining feature of the nervous system was its electrical nature, then we should have to admit that a power grid or a telephone switchboard or a television set or, again, an electronic computer, was conscious. Next we might point to the complexity of the nervous system as constituting the crucial difference. Suppose we say, to quote Ashby, that '. . . all systems in which the amount of communication exceeds, say, 10^8 bits per second should have self-awareness'. We again get into difficulties: 'Such a level might include the largest general computers and would certainly include such complex dynamic systems as the Steel Industry, the Railways of Britain, the Russian Army, the Amazon Jungle. Those who claim that the complexity of the human brain is sufficient to explain its self-awareness must be prepared either to admit that the systems above have their own "personal" self-awareness, or to give reasons for the denial.'[1]

Suppose now that on one of the grounds above we concluded that if the mammalian brain was conscious, the computer must be too. As we have seen, we should at the same time have to admit that various other systems were also conscious: e.g. toes, or television sets, or the steel industry. At the extreme we might even be led to the belief that all matter is conscious. 'At school', says Good in a provocative paper,[2] 'I once suggested that even the smallest particle of inorganic matter has a microscopic measure of consciousness, say 10^{-100} doogs, which is greatly amplified in organised systems. My schoolmates regarded this suggestion as highly risible, stupid, unbalanced, and contemptible. A similar fate befell Spinoza for similar remarks.' We might, however, say that to be conscious a system must be organic *and* electric *and* complex *and* a host of other attributes which together define uniquely the mammalian nervous system and nothing else. This is a tenable point of view, and would

[1] Ashby, op. cit., p. 312.
[2] Good, Irving J., 'The mind-body problem, or could an android feel pain?', in Scher (Ed.), op. cit.

exclude computers from the category of systems with consciousness: it would in effect define consciousness as an attribute of the mammalian nervous system and of nothing else.[1] However, if this argument is pursued a new kind of difficulty emerges.

Let us take this commonsense position that the computer does *not* possess consciousness. Now suppose also, which is consistent with the argument of previous chapters, that computers can in principle simulate all specifiable types of human behaviour (learning, problem-solving, etc.). It may take a long time for all types of behaviour to be fully simulated in practice, but it is not inconceivable that one day they will be—and that many processes will even be improved on by computer. Then it becomes apparent that consciousness is not essential for the performance of these types of behaviour. If a computer can learn, or recognise patterns, or direct its own behaviour, or develop attitudes, without consciousness, a human being could in principle do the same. And if this is the case it has to be admitted that consciousness, from the point of view of biological evolution, is superfluous: that is, it contributes nothing to the individual's chances of survival in a hostile world. Indeed, one could imagine a world, identical in all respects with our own, except that brain processes had no corresponding conscious processes. On this argument, consciousness is biologically gratuitous. Why, then, should it have emerged at all? We can hardly argue, that, like the appendix, consciousness is the vestigial remains of some process that was evolutionarily advantageous at some earlier stage of evolution. If the computer can simulate the complexities of brain processes in modern man, it should, *a fortiori*, be able to simulate the simpler brain processes of our remote ancestors—and in this case the argument used above can be re-applied to the effect that consciousness had no evolutionary purpose at that stage either.

It must be emphasised again that the term 'consciousness' as used in the last paragraph and throughout this chapter means 'subjective experience'. By contrast, if it is used in a neurophysiological sense to mean 'wakefulness' or 'attention' then it is quite reasonable to say that consciousness serves an evolutionary purpose.[2] (In this

[1] Brain, for example, seems to take something like this position when he quotes with approval another writer who says that 'the brain . . . however its functions may be mimicked by machines, remains itself and is unique in nature' (Brain, op. cit., p. 85).

[2] As an example of this sort of argument see Miller, George A., 'Thinking, cognition and learning', in Berelson, Bernard (Ed.), *The Behavioral Sciences Today* (New York. Harper Torchbooks, 1964).

sense it would also be meaningful to say that one could simulate consciousness in a computer program.) But this is *not* what this chapter has been about.

At this final stage, then, a tough-minded attitude to the computer-human comparison may have to be softened by the realisation that, when we come to the question 'Can a computer be conscious?', we are led into profound difficulties whichever way we answer it. Either we have to admit that it can be, in which case we probably also have to admit consciousness in a number of other systems which we should not normally wish to accept were conscious (and this would incidentally raise a number of ethical problems); or we deny computer-consciousness in which case we have to explain what purpose consciousness serves in human beings—and may be forced to give some sort of religious or metaphysical answer. We could avoid all these difficulties by denying the conscious aspects of our own brain processes. But who would seriously wish to do that?

IN CONCLUSION

We have now, as it were, followed the mechanist hypothesis that 'man is a machine' through to its bitter end in the morass of problems which bear upon the nature of *subjective experience*. The difficulties that arise in this respect should not, however, obscure the strength of the mechanist hypothesis as far as *objective behaviour* is concerned. The computer and related studies that have been described in this book add considerable weight to this hypothesis by showing that there would seem to be no form of human behaviour which it is in principle impossible to reproduce in machine form although such reproduction is in fact only at its beginnings. Thus we have seen that a machine is not restricted in its functioning to algorithms, but may also make use of heuristics. We have seen that a machine can produce infinitely varied behaviour (for example linguistic behaviour) on the basis of a finite set of rules. And we have seen that there is nothing inherently mysterious about purposeful, nor about emotional, behaviour, although a detailed understanding of such behaviour and its underlying physiology will no doubt have to wait on the work of many future generations of psychologists.

We have also in this book looked at examples of many different kinds of computer models, some algorithmic and others heuristic, some probabilistic and other deterministic, some intended wholly for the purpose of simulation and others at least partly for more immediately practical purposes, some derived from abstract theoretical ideas and others based primarily on observation. It should be clear that the range of models in terms of processes simulated is also fairly wide and is developing rapidly.

The achievements and shortcomings of the various models have been pointed out as they have been discussed in the text. If a general weakness is to be indicated it is that of the lack of suitable methods for determining how well the behaviour of a model matches that of the system it is modelling. Where the model and the system modelled pursue identical goals (recognising hand-written letters, playing chess, etc.) one can at least determine whether the model has achieved the required goal. In other cases, as in the models of personality, the position is more difficult because there are no clear-cut ends for the model to pursue; therefore the environment has to be simulated as well as the model, which makes the situation more arbitrary and the model more difficult to compare with human behaviour. But even where one can determine directly whether or not a certain goal has been achieved by the model there is still the main problem of deciding how far it was achieved in the same way as in the system simulated, which means that a step-by-step comparison of the behaviour of the two systems is required. This is difficult to accomplish because much of the human behaviour may be covert, and the use of protocols (for example by Newell, Simon and Shaw) as evidence is a questionable procedure. (This is of course because there is no way to determine how accurate a representation of someone's thoughts a verbal protocol is, and thinking aloud in any case affect the thinking process itself.) Again, even if one has step-by-step evidence how does one decide how similar two systems are? Turing's test is almost certainly too weak but more precise methods, as Feldman found (Chapter 5), also run into difficulties. There is every sign that this urgent problem is receiving increasing attention from those working in the field.

Assuming that this problem can be overcome, how useful is the technique of computer simulation likely to be in psychology in the future? There are of course ways of modelling other than by means of computers, and ways of theorising other than by means of models. Nevertheless if operational definitions and controlled experiments can be combined with effective computer models associated with rigorous higher-level theories of a cybernetic variety, then there is every chance that psychology can develop as a tough-minded science which is also willing to recognise the richness and complexity and purposefulness of human behaviour. In this way it should be possible to take the best of both the Gestalt and the Behaviourist schools, accepting the importance of organisation in behaviour as well as the necessity to use objective experimental methods. It also means that one can be centralist rather than peripheralist without being imprecise: one can use cognitive concepts like those of Tolman ('expectancies', etc.) without losing any of the systematic rigour of a Hull.

To adapt Chomsky's terminology, it is not enough to look at the surface structure of behaviour: somehow we have to infer the deep structure. The organism organises—and we must try to understand the principles of this organisation. What is sometimes called the 'empty organism' is in reality a 'full organism' and a highly complex one at that. The importance of the advent of computers is that it provides a systematic way of making inferences about the deep structure, about the competence which is necessary for a system to produce complex behaviour of the kind produced by human beings. In its own way, and despite its various disadvantages, the computer may prove in the long run to be as important to psychology as the telescope has been to astronomy and the microscope to biology.

SELECTED REFERENCES

Anderson, Alan Ross (Ed.), *Minds and Machines* (New Jersey, Prentice-Hall, 1964).

Eccles, J. C. (Ed.), *Brain and Conscious Experience* (Heidelberg, Springer, 1966).

Hook, Sidney (Ed.), *Dimensions of Mind* (New York, Collier Books, 1961).

Reeves, Joan Wynn, *Body and Mind in Western Thought* (London, Penguin Books, 1958).

Ryle, Gilbert, *The Concept of Mind* (London, Hutchinson, 1949; Penguin Books, 1963).

Scher, Jordan (Ed.), *Theories of the Mind* (New York, Macmillan, 1962).

Sluckin, W., *Minds and Machines* (London, Penguin Books, 1954).

FURTHER READING

Andrew, A. M., *Brains and Computers* (London, Harrap, 1963).
Borko, Harold (Ed.), *Computer Applications in the Behavioral Sciences* (New Jersey, Prentice-Hall, 1962).
Feigenbaum, Edward A., and Feldman, Julian (Eds.), *Computers and Thought* (New York, McGraw-Hill, 1963).
Fink, Donald G., *Computers and the Human Mind* (London, Heinemann, 1968).
George, F. H., *The Brain as a Computer* (Oxford, Pergamon, 1961) and *Models of Thinking* (London, George Allen and Unwin, 1970).
Hunt, Earl, 'Computer simulation: artificial intelligence studies and their relevance to psychology', in *Annual Review of Psychology* (1968), vol. 19, Farnsworth, P. R., Ed. (California, Annual Reviews Inc., 1968).
Loehlin, John C., *Computer Models of Personality* (New York, Random House, 1968).
Science Journal, Machines like Men (special issue October 1968), vol. 4, no. 10.
Scientific American: Mathematical Thinking in the Behavioral Sciences (New York, Freeman and Co., 1968).
Sluckin, W., *Minds and Machines* (London, Penguin Books, 1954).
Tomkins, Silvan S., and Messik, Samuel, *Computer Simulation of Personality* (New York, Wiley, 1963).

INDEX

Page numbers in **bold** refer to names that occur in the 'Selected References' at the end of chapters and 'Further Reading' at the end of the book.